C000203164

FIG TREE

Published by the Penguin Group
Penguin Books Ltd, 80 Strand, London WC2R 0RL, England
Penguin Group (USA) Inc., 375 Hudson Street, New York, New York 10014, USA
Penguin Group (Canada), 90 Eglinton Avenue East, Suite 700, Toronto, Ontario, Canada M4P 2Y3
(a division of Pearson Penguin Canada Inc.)
Penguin Ireland, 25 St Stephen's Green, Dublin 2, Ireland (a division of Penguin Books Ltd)
Penguin Group (Australia), 707 Collins Street,
Melbourne, Victoria 3008, Australia (a division of Pearson Australia Group Pty Ltd)
Penguin Books India Pvt Ltd, 11 Community Centre,
Panchsheel Park, New Delhi – 110 017, India
Penguin Group (NZ), 67 Apollo Drive, Rosedale, Auckland 0632, New Zealand
(a division of Pearson New Zealand Ltd)
Penguin Books (South Africa) (Pty) Ltd, 24 Sturdee Avenue,
Rosebank, Johannesburg 2196, South Africa

Penguin Books Ltd, Registered Offices: 80 Strand, London WC2R 0RL, England

www.penguin.com

First published 2011
004

www.greenpenguin.co.uk

Penguin Random House is committed to a
sustainable future for our business, our readers
and our planet. This book is made from Forest
Stewardship Council® certified paper.

Copyright © Sam and Eddie Hart and Nieves Barragán Mohacho, 2011
Photography copyright © Emma Lee, 2011
Design by Nathan Burton

The moral right of the authors has been asserted

All rights reserved
Without limiting the rights under copyright
reserved above, no part of this publication may be
reproduced, stored in or introduced into a retrieval system,
or transmitted, in any form or by any means (electronic, mechanical,
photocopying, recording or otherwise), without the prior
written permission of both the copyright owner and
the above publisher of this book

Printed in China. Colour reproduction by Altaimage Ltd

A CIP catalogue record for this book is available from the British Library

ISBN: 978-1-905-49074-5

BARRAFINA
A SPANISH COOKBOOK

SAM AND EDDIE HART
AND
NIEVES BARRAGÁN MOHACHO

FIG TREE
an imprint of
PENGUIN BOOKS

- 2 OXTAIL + SCALLOP

- 1 Pig CHEEKS

- ~~FRITURA~~

- ~~BEETROOT SALAD~~

$5 LITTLE SERVING OF
THE SEAFOOD RICE
PLS!

MICHAEL

CONTENTS

INTRODUCTION 7

PARA PICAR 23

COLD MEATS 43

FISH AND SEAFOOD 45

MEAT 111

TORTILLA 165

SALADS AND VEGETABLES 173

SAUCES, STOCKS AND BASICS 205

DESSERTS 219

LIST OF SUPPLIERS 244

INDEX 246

ACKNOWLEDGEMENTS 255

INTRODUCTION

Our mother grew up on the Balearic island of Mallorca. Although by blood she is the slightly rare combination of Bulgarian and Scottish, she grew up living the life of a Mallorquín village girl. Our grandfather built a house in the tiny village of Estellencs, on the northwest coast, and we are lucky enough to have kept hold of it ever since. We have spent most of our summers in Mallorca since we were born, and this, combined with the Spanish influence of our mother at home, has instilled in us a great love of the country and its cuisine. Food in Mallorca is simple, but authentic and delicious. There are wonderful markets selling everything from local lamb to weaver wrasse, a highly prized fish that appears only during the month of August. There are always a multitude of members of the family willing and able to cook the lunch or dinner, and none are exempt from interference of one kind or another from the others. We tend not to venture very far from our village, which is quite remote, but scattered up and down the coast are some first-rate, if simple restaurants. The uniting factor of these humble establishments is that they use brilliant raw ingredients and do very little to them. Our passion for Spanish

cuisine was born from summers spent enjoying the flavours of what was in season: roasted peppers and aubergines, mountain lamb and fish caught just off the coast.

Our appreciation of Spanish gastronomy grew still further when Eddie spent a year living in Madrid as a young student in the early 1990s. He lived with an unemployed Spanish gastronome who would spend his days playing cards and teaching Eddie to cook tortilla and croquetas. Sam lived in Barcelona for six months as part of a plan to continue his early career as a nightclub entrepreneur. Happily the nightclub project didn't progress much, and he spent his days idly wandering around the splendid Boqueria market looking for inspiration as to what to have for lunch.

It was while Sam was living in Barcelona that we came across the now legendary Cal Pep, in the El Born district of the city. Beyond a narrow door on a slightly scruffy square was a tiny L-shaped bar with twenty-three seats and all the cooking going on behind it. Holding court was the gravelly-voiced Pep himself, directing operations with a rod of iron. There was no menu, and the customers would just ask the waiter what there was that day and order accordingly. The food, mostly fish and seafood but some meat as well, was brilliant. Perfectly fresh and using wonderful ingredients, it was prepared with the utmost simplicity. Simple here does not mean easy or slapdash. Every dish that came from the kitchen was expertly and precisely cooked, and if you are not hiding behind complicated sauces that is a difficult thing to do. Every time a customer finished their food and left there was another to take their place – the atmosphere was electric. Needless to say, having eaten almost all the menu and drunk half the cellar we were hooked.

This was back in 2000, and at the time London was desperately short of good Spanish restaurants, particularly tapas restaurants. After several more visits to Pep and travels around the rest of Spain (for research purposes mostly), eating at some other excellent places, we decided that a Cal Pep was what London needed in its gastronomic life. We searched and scoured central London for suitable venues as we set about fine-tuning our project. The more we thought about it the more we began to believe that London, with no high-class tapas restaurants, was not quite ready to go the whole – bar only, no tables, no reservations – hog. We instead opted for a restaurant with tables and chairs as normal, but with a large bar counter for our customers to eat overlooking a semi-open kitchen. That was Fino and the year was 2003.

Our first head chef at Fino, a brilliant Frenchman, Jean-Philippe Patruno, who now runs the kitchen at Barrafina's sister restaurant, Quo Vadis, knew of a Spanish sous-chef and suggested we try to poach her. We succeeded, and Nieves Barragán came to work for us two months before Fino opened. Four years passed, with Nieves working alongside Jean-Philippe at Fino, and it was beginning to become obvious to us that she was ready to take charge of a kitchen herself. It didn't take us too long to decide that what we wanted to do was return to our original idea and create a London Cal Pep, with no tables, no reservations, and all the cooking done behind the bar as close to the customer as possible and with everything on display, warts and all.

A site became available on Frith Street, in the middle of Soho, the right size for what we wanted, and we were off. We would water down the concept only by the inclusion of a printed menu (which also became our place mat). However, this would be supplemented by a selection of daily specials that would only be communicated by word of mouth, although most (the delicious seafood) would be on display on a bed of ice behind the bar.

Waiters and chefs are not used to sharing the same space, particularly not a very small (1.5 metres at its widest) corridor while in the middle of a busy service. At the beginning tempers flared as the different parties crashed into, pushed and stepped on each other. As the months went by, however, a delicate dance began to take place behind the bar, with the kitchen and waiters deftly and gracefully working within the confines of the space.

The problem with having no reservations is that you can arrive for your lunch or dinner only to discover that all the seats have been taken. We therefore decided to have a shelf behind the bar seats where it would be possible to wait and have a drink and something to nibble on. It struck us that if the queue were to work and people were to keep good-humoured, two important factors would have to be adhered to. First, that the queue should move steadily in one direction so that it had a front and a back, rather than giving people a number and calling them when their seats were ready. This means that the customers can gauge their progress by their steady movement in the right direction. The next and most important factor to us about the queue was that there would be no queue-barging, ever, no matter how important the customer. We are very proud to have stuck to this principle without exception ever since we first opened. A-list Hollywood film stars, restaurant critics, business leaders and politicians, even our own mother, have to wait in line with everyone else. You might say that the system works in a dual culture of no reservations (a rather Spanish thing), with orderly queuing (a very British state of affairs)!

Once in command of her own kitchen Nieves really flourished. Nieves grew up in and around Bilbao, in the Basque Country. The Basques are famous for their dedication to the culinary arts, and Nieves's home was no exception. Her grandmother lived with the family and was paralysed down one side of her body, which meant it was difficult for Nieves's mother to leave the house. To entertain Nieves her mother involved her in the cooking, starting with peeling potatoes and stirring the occasional pan, and progressing on to roasting a chicken at the tender age of seven. Nieves discovered a passion for food from a very early age, and whether shopping with her mother in the local markets or cooking for family and friends, food was never far from her mind. This was not fancy food, but considerable time and effort were put into the sourcing and careful preparation of excellent local ingredients. At Barrafina we do not cook only Basque food; however, the influence of that part of Spain can be seen in much of what we do.

The food at Barrafina has, in our completely biased opinion, got steadily better ever since we opened. With the daily specials inspiring constant creativity, the wonderful new dishes keep on coming and our ever-increasing number of regulars keep on coming back for more. As those of you who know us are already aware, we are not chefs ourselves but keep in very close contact with our chefs in discussing new dishes, improvements to old dishes, suppliers and menus.

In this book Nieves has taken us through her dishes step by step and we have dutifully transcribed her methods, adapting where necessary for the home cook rather than the professional chef. We hope you enjoy both cooking and eating them as much as we do.

A NOTE ON COOKING

Cooking, with the exception of baking, is not an exact science. Every piece of meat or fish, every oven and every pan, is slightly different from the last. We have taken real care to give as precise instructions as possible regarding quantities, cooking times and methods. However, the most important part of cooking is not following the recipe but using your senses – taste, sight, touch and smell. Tiny variations can make all the difference between good and brilliant. Try to taste as much as you can as you go along, so as to have the seasoning and cuisson just so.

DEEP-FRYING

The Spanish are the masters of deep-frying, and it would be remiss of us not to include a certain amount of it in this book. There are a few points worth noting:

1. It is vital to use plenty of clean oil – 1 litre should generally do it. Ideally you would use pomace olive oil, but sunflower or vegetable oil will do.

2. Make sure the oil is at 180°C before you start to cook. The food will become greasy if the oil is not hot enough. If you have a deep-fryer at home it should have a temperature gauge built in, but if you don't have one you can heat the oil over a medium heat in a large deep pan and check the temperature with a cook's thermometer. It is vital that the oil remains at the precise temperature of 180°C, so make sure you check it regularly.

3. Deep-frying does give off a certain aroma. Apart from all the obvious tricks of switching on the extraction fan and opening windows, we have developed a smoke-free method for the home cook, which just needs a little outdoor space. We connect our deep-fryer to a lengthy extension lead and take the whole thing out into the garden – but make sure it is not raining. You can then fry out in the open air to your heart's content and leave your house odour-free!

ABOUT SHOPPING

The food in Barrafina is all about good ingredients prepared simply. It is very important that you try to source the best quality of raw produce possible. Very few of the dishes work with substandard meat, fish or veg.

A FEW ESSENTIALS

There are a few ingredients we use that are very specific, and while there are, I am sure, excellent alternatives, for the authentic taste of Barrafina the following are really worth seeking out. You can find them all online, or from the suppliers that we list on page 244.

EXTRA VIRGIN OLIVE OIL
This is such an important part of Spanish cooking that it is really important to source something good. Arbequina is a native Spanish olive and quite peppery. We use Brindisa's Arbequina olive oil.

SHERRY VINEGAR
There are many lamentable sherry vinegars on the market, and in a dressing that consists only of oil and vinegar its quality is vital. We use the wonderful Valdespino sherry vinegar.

MOSCATEL VINEGAR
Made from the slightly sweet Moscatel grape, this is a brilliant light vinegar. We use Unio Moscatel vinegar.

PX BALSAMIC VINEGAR
Aged balsamic vinegar from Pedro Ximénez grapes, dark and syrupy and with a wonderful depth of flavour. We use PX Balsamic Sotaroni 8 year. In our recipes we often use a Pedro Ximénez reduction, which we make by simmering the vinegar until it has reduced by two-thirds.

SALT
We use only Maldon salt. It has a much gentler flavour than normal salt.

SPECIAL FLOUR FOR FRYING
This is a coarse flour from Andalucía, designed specifically for frying fish. It gives a delicious crunch and doesn't absorb much oil. We use Harina Especial para Freir by Panaeras. It is difficult to find in the UK at the moment, but City Meat on the King's Road in London usually stock it – see our list of suppliers on page 244. If you can't obtain the special flour, try a mixture of half breadcrumbs and half plain flour, which works quite well.

JUANOLAS
These are little liquorice drops that we use to make a sauce for strawberries and are available online – try www.confitelia.com. and see our list of suppliers on page 244.

SAFFRON
The quality of saffron varies enormously. The best are the Spanish rather than the Oriental brands.

CURED MEATS

We use only 'Ibérico' cold meats. 'Ibérico' meat is produced from the black-footed Iberian pig, fattened, free-range, on a diet of acorns. 'Ibérico' is an excellent badge of quality, and although of course there are differences, most 'Ibérico' products should be good. Iberian meats are available from good delicatessens and Spanish food stores.

PIQUILLO PEPPERS

Piquillo peppers are roasted red peppers from Navarra in northern Spain. These slightly sweet, non-spicy peppers are wood-roasted, then peeled by hand and tinned. They keep very well in tins and are a great cook's shortcut, as the roasting and peeling process would otherwise take the best part of an hour. They are available from Spanish and other good delicatessens.

PAPRIKA

There are three kinds of paprika used in this book: sweet, smoked, and smoked and spicy. They give a wonderful depth of flavour to all sorts of Spanish dishes and are vital to Spanish cuisine.

CHORICERO PEPPERS

These are dried red chillies, about the size of a hand. They are slightly smoky and only a little spicy. You reconstitute them by soaking them in warm water for 30 minutes before using them in stews.

ALMONDS

We use Marcona almonds from Aragón. They are widely considered to be the best, but unfortunately this means they are not cheap. However, they are extremely delicious and well worth the extra expense.

OLIVES

We use a mixture of different olives at Barrafina, a combination of sizes, textures and flavours.

RICE

The Spanish use two main strains of rice for paellas and other rice dishes: Bomba and Calasparra. They have similar properties, although we tend to use Calasparra because it has a slightly longer, more elegant grain.

CALÇOTS

Calçots are a cross between a spring onion and a leek, and are a Catalan delicacy eaten in the early spring. Booth's of Borough Market (see page 244) is the only supplier we have come across in the UK. Substitute large spring onions if you cannot find calçots.

WHITE ASPARAGUS

The Spanish are very keen on white asparagus and eat it both fresh, from a good greengrocer, or tinned.

TOMATE FRITO

Tomate frito is a pre-made blitzed sauce of tomatoes fried in olive oil with a little garlic and onion. You can buy it in bottles from specialist shops. If you can't find tomate frito, Italian passata will work as a substitute.

MOJAMA

Mojama is wind-dried tuna made on the southern Atlantic coast in Spanish towns such as Zahara de los Atunes. It has a strong, salty taste and is excellent at adding oomph to more delicate dishes. You buy it in a block and very thinly slice or grate it over a finished dish.

SHERRY

To say we are mad about sherry is an understatement, and we have always promoted this hugely under-appreciated, fortified wine. With so many different styles of sherry available, there are wines that are perfect as an aperitif, with fish and shellfish, with meat and game and with dessert. Our favourite styles are:

MANZANILLA
A light, dry, salty and yeasty wine from Sanlúcar de Barrameda – aperitif, seafood and shellfish.

FINO
Slightly weightier and nuttier than manzanilla but still bone dry – aperitif, seafood and shellfish.

MANZANILLA PASADA
An aged manzanilla, this style tends to be extremely complex and dry – aperitif, seafood, shellfish and poultry.

AMONTILLADO
Much darker in colour, with flavours of caramelized nuts, raisins, figs and spice and a hint of saltiness – aperitif, poultry and game.

PALO CORTADO
A rare and complex wine with intense nutty aromas and long, lingering flavours – aperitif, poultry and game.

DRY OLOROSO
Rich in colour, with orange citrus peel notes and spice; nutty and very expressive – aperitif, particularly before Sunday lunch.

OLOROSO DULCE/SEMIDULCE
This is oloroso sweetened with Pedro Ximénez and ranges from off dry to quite sweet. We find it a brilliant accompaniment to Santiago Tart or Spanish cheeses.

PEDRO XIMÉNEZ
This unique sun-dried grape produces prodigiously sweet and concentrated wine. Fans of PX adore it, and swear by its ability to be paired with dark chocolate.

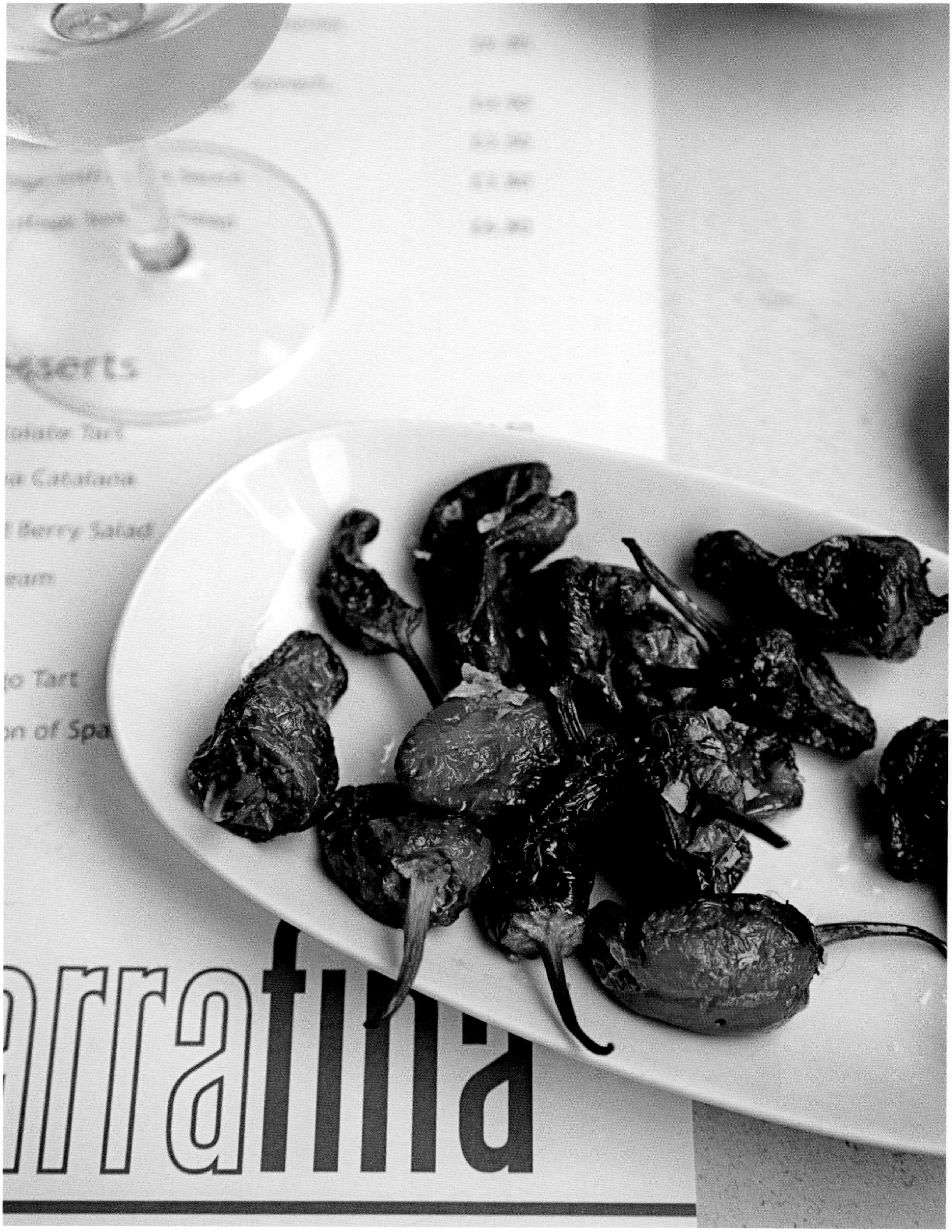
Catalana
Berry Salad
arrafina

PARA PICAR

'Para picar' means 'for picking at', and all these recipes are designed to be eaten with your hands, with drinks or as an informal starter. At Barrafina we serve the Para Picar menu in the queue, to keep the wolf from the door while you wait for a stool at the bar. You'll find quite a few fried dishes in this section, simply because fried food is perfect to pick at with a drink.

MARINATED OLIVES

100g Gordal olives
100g Aragón olives
100g Manzanilla olives
1 garlic clove, peeled and finely sliced
3 bay leaves, fresh if possible
1 teaspoon fresh thyme leaves
juice of 1 lemon
juice of 1 orange
1 tablespoon extra virgin olive oil
1 teaspoon sweet smoked paprika

We use a mixture of three classic Spanish olive varieties for this dish, but feel free to improvise with whichever olives you prefer. It is nice, however, to have a mixture of black, green, large and small. The marinated olives will keep happily in the fridge for 2 to 3 days.

SERVES 4–6 AS A TAPA

Put all the ingredients into a bowl and mix, then leave to marinate in the fridge overnight.
    Allow the olives to return to room temperature before serving.

PIMIENTOS DE PADRÓN

A few years ago you could only find pimientos de Padrón, the delicious peppers from the town of Padrón in Galicia, in specialist Spanish delicatessens. Happily this is not the case any more, as many of the major supermarkets now stock them. We cannot think of a more delicious snack, or one that is easier to produce.

SERVES 4 AS A TAPA

100ml good-quality olive oil
200g pimientos de Padrón
(about 25 peppers)
Maldon salt

Heat the oil in a sauté pan or a heavy-bottomed frying pan over a high heat until almost smoking, then reduce the heat to medium and add the peppers. Cook for 2 to 3 minutes, until they start to blister. Remove from the pan and drain on kitchen paper.
    Transfer the peppers to a plate and sprinkle liberally with Maldon salt before serving.

PAN CON TOMATE

It's all about the ingredients here – good tomatoes, good extra virgin olive oil and good bread. At Barrafina we use the white sourdough that we bake at our sister restaurant, Quo Vadis, just round the corner.

SERVES 4 AS A TAPA

4 slices of white sourdough bread, 2cm thick
1 garlic clove, peeled and halved
8–12 plum tomatoes, halved
4 tablespoons extra virgin olive oil
Maldon salt and freshly ground black pepper
1 tablespoon chopped fresh flat-leaf parsley

Lightly toast the bread on both sides and rub each slice with the cut side of the garlic.

Using your hands, squeeze 2 or 3 tomatoes over each slice so that the juice and pips fall on to the toasted bread.

Drizzle a tablespoon of olive oil over each slice. Season well with salt and pepper and sprinkle with a little chopped parsley before serving.

White Wine

Alquézar 2009
Somontano – Macabeo
Light exotic fruit, elegant

Palacio de Vive
Rueda – Verdejo
Fresh and floral with

Basa 2009
Rueda – Sauv
Notes of green fr

Monterrei, G
Fruity aromas

Muga 2
Rioja

BROAD BEANS AND GOAT'S CHEESE ON TOAST

This is a great summery starter or light meal. Shelling and skinning the broad beans is time-consuming, but in our opinion essential for the dish to be successful. If you don't have any chicken stock to hand, replace it with water or even a good dash of manzanilla sherry.

SERVES 4 AS A TAPA

12 tablespoons Pedro Ximénez balsamic vinegar
8 tablespoons good-quality olive oil
2 large onions, peeled and finely chopped
2 tablespoons fresh thyme leaves
500g Mont Enebro (or other mild goat's cheese log), skin removed
Maldon salt and freshly ground black pepper
200g fresh broad beans (shelled weight – about 2kg before shelling)
3 whole garlic cloves, peeled
4 slices of sourdough bread, 2cm thick
1 large shallot, peeled and finely diced
50ml Chicken Stock (see page 208)
4 fresh mint leaves, finely sliced
extra virgin olive oil, for finishing

Put the Pedro Ximénez balsamic vinegar into a small pan and bring to the boil. Reduce the heat and simmer until it has reduced by two-thirds, to 4 tablespoons.

Heat 4 tablespoons of olive oil in a heavy-bottomed frying pan over a medium heat. Add the onions and cook gently for 30 to 35 minutes, stirring regularly to prevent them sticking. Add the thyme leaves, then remove from the heat and set aside to cool a little.

Crumble the goat's cheese into a blender or food processor and add the caramelized onions plus a few grinds of black pepper. Blitz well and set aside.

Blanch the beans in a large pan of boiling water for 1 minute, then drain them and plunge them into a bowl of iced water. When cool, drain again and set aside.

Heat 2 tablespoons of olive oil in a heavy-bottomed frying pan and toast the bread on both sides until golden. Remove from the pan, then halve one of the garlic cloves and rub the cut edges over one side of each bread slice. Finely slice the other 2 garlic cloves.

In the pan used for the toast, heat 2 tablespoons of olive oil. Add the sliced garlic and diced shallot and cook gently for 2 to 3 minutes, until they start to colour. Add the beans, then add the stock and simmer for 2 minutes, until the liquid has almost evaporated. Add the mint and remove from the heat.

Spread the cheese mixture generously over each slice of toast. Spoon the beans on top, season and drizzle with extra virgin olive oil and the Pedro Ximénez reduction.

CHIPIRONES

Chipirones, also known as puntillitas in Spain, are crisp fried baby squid and are served as a tapa in almost every bar. We stray from the traditional a little here by adding finely diced garlic and thyme leaves, which we think gives another dimension to the dish. Chipirones are so small that you do not need to clean them, just rinse them very well under running cold water. If you can't find baby squid, you can use small squid sliced into rings.

SERVES 4 AS A TAPA

1 litre oil for deep-frying
450g baby squid
200g special flour for frying (see page 17)
1 garlic clove, peeled and finely chopped
1 teaspoon fresh thyme leaves
Maldon salt and freshly ground black pepper
1 lemon, cut into quarters

Heat the oil to 180°C in a large pan or a deep-fryer. Place the baby squid in a bowl in the sink and rinse them gently under running water, to remove any traces of grit. Drain and dry well on kitchen paper.

Put the special flour into a large bowl. Add the baby squid and toss in the flour, coating them well. Fry them in the oil for 2 to 3 minutes, until crisp, then remove them from the oil and drain on plenty of kitchen paper.

Put the fried baby squid into a large bowl and add the garlic, thyme leaves, pepper and plenty of salt. Serve with the lemon quarters and eat at once, while still piping hot.

DELICIAS

Delicias by name, delicious by nature! These are the Spanish equivalent of the 1970s English classic 'Devils on Horseback', and traditionally come from the town of Elche, inland from Alicante. They differ from their British cousins in being stuffed with almonds and fried until crisp. At Barrafina we serve them with a little watercress salad.

SERVES 4 AS A TAPA

12 Marcona almonds
12 large pitted dates
6 thin slices of smoked pancetta
1 small shallot, peeled and finely chopped
2 tablespoons olive oil
2 tablespoons Moscatel vinegar
a bunch of watercress
Maldon salt
olive oil, for frying

Stuff an almond into the centre of each date. Cut each slice of pancetta in half, then wrap each date with a piece of pancetta and secure with a toothpick. Repeat with the rest of the dates.

In a bowl whisk together the chopped shallot, olive oil and vinegar. Add the watercress, season with salt and mix well.

Heat about 1cm of olive oil in a heavy-bottomed frying pan and fry the dates on all sides, until the pancetta is brown and crisp. Alternatively you can heat oil to 180°C in a deep-fryer and deep-fry the dates for 30 seconds.

Serve at once, with the watercress salad.

CRISP FRIED ANCHOVIES

This is one of our favourite dishes, best eaten really hot with your fingers. At Barrafina it is interesting to observe the different eating methods employed by our clientele – from the prudish, carefully slicing each fillet from the tiny bones, to the adventurous, who cheerfully guzzle down the whole fish, head, bones and all.

SERVES 4 AS A TAPA

1 litre oil for deep-frying
500g fresh anchovies (around 25–35)
220g special flour for frying
(see page 17)
Maldon salt
1 lemon, cut into quarters

Heat the oil to 180°C in a large pan or a deep-fryer. Gut each anchovy by running your finger down the belly and gently pulling out the insides. Wash the little fish under lots of cold running water and carefully pat dry.

Put the flour on to a plate. Dust the fish in the flour and fry in batches in the oil for 2 to 3 minutes. Remove from the pan and drain on kitchen paper.

Season liberally with Maldon salt and serve with the lemon quarters.

HAM CROQUETAS

These are particularly delicious. We have been tinkering around with the recipe over the years and feel that this is now as close to perfection as we can get. They are slightly fiddly to make, so you will probably want to keep them for special occasions.

MAKES ABOUT 30 CROQUETAS

250g good-quality Serrano ham, in one piece
4 dessertspoons olive oil
120g unsalted butter
115g plain flour
1 litre full-fat milk
½ teaspoon grated nutmeg
Maldon salt and freshly ground black pepper
3 free-range eggs, beaten
250g breadcrumbs
1 litre oil for deep-frying

Cut the ham into 0.5cm cubes. Heat the oil and butter in a large, heavy-bottomed pan and gently fry the ham for about 10 minutes, until any fat has been largely rendered off. Stir in the flour and continue to cook over a low heat for a further 10 minutes, stirring frequently.

Put the milk into a pan and gently warm it to just below a simmer. Gradually beat the warm milk into the ham and flour mixture, stirring all the time to form a smooth béchamel. Continue to cook and stir for a further 10 to 15 minutes. Add the nutmeg and season with salt and pepper.

Remove from the heat, transfer the mixture to a container and leave to cool slightly. Cover with cling-film, pressing it down on to the surface of the béchamel to prevent a skin forming. Put into the fridge for a minimum of 4 hours.

To make the croquetas, arrange a little production line: first the container of béchamel, then the beaten eggs in a shallow bowl, followed by the breadcrumbs in another shallow bowl, and lastly a tray for the finished croquetas. Using your hands, form a golfball-sized sphere with the béchamel. Dip it into the egg, coat well with the breadcrumbs and leave to rest on the tray. Repeat with the rest of the mixture.

Heat the oil to 180°C in a large pan or a deep-fryer and fry the croquetas in batches for about 2 to 3 minutes, until heated through and golden brown. Remove from the oil, drain on kitchen paper and serve at once, while still good and hot!

PRAWN CROQUETAS

As a fishy alternative to ham croquetas, these work very well indeed. Better, perhaps, than the ham if you are already eating a lot of pork elsewhere in the meal.

MAKES ABOUT 30 CROQUETAS

1 tablespoon olive oil
300g raw peeled medium prawns, cut into 1.5cm chunks
120g butter
115g plain flour
500ml milk
500ml Bisque (see page 211)
3 dessertspoons chopped fresh chives
Maldon salt and freshly ground black pepper
3 free-range eggs, beaten
250g breadcrumbs
1 litre oil for deep-frying

Heat the olive oil in a large, heavy-bottomed pan and gently fry the prawns for a few minutes until pink and cooked through. Remove them from the oil and set aside. In the same pan gently melt the butter, then stir in the flour and cook gently for 15 minutes, stirring regularly.

In a separate pan warm the milk and the bisque. Gradually beat the warm milk and bisque into the flour mixture, stirring all the time to form a smooth béchamel. Continue to cook and stir for another 10 minutes or so, or until the mixture is quite thick. Add the prawns and chives and mix well. Season liberally with salt and pepper.

Remove from the heat, transfer to a container and leave to cool slightly. Cover with clingfilm, pressing it down on to the surface of the béchamel to prevent a skin forming. Put into the fridge for a minimum of 4 hours.

To make the croquetas, arrange a little production line: first the container of béchamel, then the beaten eggs in a shallow bowl, followed by the breadcrumbs in another shallow bowl, and lastly a tray for the finished croquetas. Using your hands, form a golfball-sized sphere with the béchamel. Dip it into the egg, coat well with the breadcrumbs and leave to rest on the tray. Repeat with the rest of the mixture.

Heat the oil to 180°C in a large pan or a deep-fryer and fry the croquetas in batches for about 2 to 3 minutes, until heated through and golden brown. Remove from the oil, drain on kitchen paper and serve immediately.

OCTOPUS WITH CAPERS

People often consider octopus to be tough, but if cooked well it is nothing of the sort. One of the great things about octopus is that it is actually improved by freezing, which makes it relatively easy to get hold of. We have departed from tradition here with the addition of capers, which we feel give a welcome acidity to the dish. The method below has a certain madness to it, but Nieves's mother, a great authority on the subject, is certain that it makes a difference.

SERVES 8 AS A TAPA

1 large double-suckered octopus, frozen (about 3.5–5kg)
1 large white onion, peeled and sliced
1 bay leaf, fresh if possible
500ml olive oil
50ml extra virgin olive oil
80g capers
2 tablespoons paprika
salt and freshly ground black pepper
2 tablespoons chopped fresh flat-leaf parsley

First, defrost the octopus. Then fill the largest pan or casserole you have with salted water and bring to the boil.

Dip the octopus 3 times into the boiling water, for 3 seconds each time, then place it in the boiling water with the head facing upwards and reduce the water to a simmer. Add the onion and bay leaf and cook for 1 hour, then turn the octopus over so that the head is facing down towards the bottom of the pan and cook for a further 30 minutes.

Take the octopus out of the water and allow to cool on a tray or draining board. Slice the tentacles into 0.5cm rounds and discard the head.

Heat the 500ml of olive oil to 80°C in a large, heavy-bottomed frying pan and fry the pieces of octopus for 2 to 3 minutes – you will need to do this in two batches. Remove from the oil and drain well.

To serve, arrange the octopus prettily on a wooden board or serving plate while still warm. Drizzle with the extra virgin olive oil and scatter the capers over. Sprinkle with paprika, season with salt and pepper and finally sprinkle with the chopped parsley.

SALT COD FRITTERS WITH TARTARE SAUCE

Fifteen years ago, our family friend Jean-Michel produced the most delicious salt cod fritters at his house near Estellencs. It was only this year that we were able to prise the recipe from him. With a few tweaks, we have recreated the fritters in Barrafina. Best eaten as a snack with cold sherry or beer.

FOR THE FRITTERS
500g salt cod
3 eggs
100ml lager
140g plain flour
3g fresh yeast, dissolved in
1 tablespoon warm water
a bunch of fresh flat-leaf parsley,
finely chopped
2 large red chillies, finely chopped
Maldon salt and freshly
ground black pepper
2 bay leaves, fresh if possible
½ an onion, peeled
1 litre oil for deep-frying

FOR THE TARTARE SAUCE
2 free-range egg yolks
2 teaspoons Dijon mustard
125ml light olive oil
125ml vegetable oil
1 shallot, peeled and very finely chopped
20g capers, drained and chopped
20g cocktail gherkins,
drained and chopped
juice of ½ a lemon
1 hard-boiled egg, chopped
1½ tablespoons finely chopped
flat-leaf parsley

SERVES 4 AS A TAPA

Put the salt cod into a bowl of cold water and refrigerate for 24 hours, changing the water 3 times. Drain, then spread it out on kitchen paper and pat dry. Remove any skin and bones that may remain.

Crack the eggs into a large mixing bowl. Add the lager and flour and whisk well until smooth. Add the yeast, parsley and chillies and season with salt and pepper. Refrigerate for at least 2 hours.

In a large pan, bring 2 litres of water to the boil with the bay leaves and onion. Add the pieces of cod and blanch for 2 to 3 minutes, then remove and drain.

Break the cod up with your hands and add to the refrigerated egg and flour mixture, stirring well. Allow to cool, then cover and refrigerate for another 2 hours.

To make the tartare sauce, whisk the egg yolks and mustard together in a bowl. Mix the oils and gradually drizzle into the egg yolks, whisking continuously to form an emulsion. When all the oil is incorporated, add the shallot, capers and gherkins. Add the lemon juice and mix well, and finally stir in the chopped hard-boiled egg and parsley and season with salt and pepper. Refrigerate until needed.

Heat the oil to 180°C in a large deep pan. Drop heaped teaspoons of the salt cod mixture into the oil and fry for 3 to 4 minutes, or until golden brown. Remove from the oil, drain on kitchen paper, season with salt and pepper and serve with the tartare sauce.

od

Plancha

Cape

llo

ish Cheeses

£4.

£4.00

£5.50

£4.50

£4.50

£4

£

barrafina

e of 12.5% will be added to
de VAT at 17.50%
any dietary requirements

COLD MEATS

Spain makes some of the best cured meats in the world, and every Spaniard will have their favourite to nibble on before the meal really begins. At Barrafina all our cold meats are Ibérico, which means they come from the black-footed Iberian pig which is fattened, free-range, on a diet of acorns. You can serve as many or as few of these as you like, and some good bread and olive oil or Pan con Tomate (see page 26) would be the perfect accompaniment. You can buy Ibérico meats from good delicatessens and some of the better supermarkets.

50G IS ENOUGH FOR 4 PEOPLE TO HAVE A LITTLE

CHORIZO IBÉRICO
A cured pork sausage that is flavoured with paprika and garlic and comes either 'curada', which can be eaten as it is, or 'semi curada', designed for cooking. Chorizo is also available spicy.

LOMO IBÉRICO
The cured loin of the Iberian pig. The least fatty of all the cold meats.

SALCHICHÓN IBÉRICO
A cured sausage but this time with no paprika.

JAMÓN IBÉRICO
The king of Spanish cold meats, this is the cured leg of Iberian pork. We slice it off the bone in Barrafina, but you can buy it pre-sliced.

PALETILLA IBÉRICO
This is the cured shoulder of pork and is often slightly fattier than the jamón.

CECINA
Cured beef from León, in northern Spain. Similar in style to the Italian bresaola – but being Spanish it is obviously much better!

FUET DE CATALUNYA
This is a thin-gauge sausage with a firmer texture than salchichón and slightly less garlicky.

MORCILLA CURADA
Cured blood sausage, for eating as you might fully cured chorizo.

MORCILLA CHORICERA
A half morcilla, half chorizo mix.

MORCILLA DE BURGOS
Blood sausage with rice and onions.

SOBRESADA DE MALLORCA
A soft chorizo with the consistency of rillettes. This is a bit of an acquired taste, but to the Mallorquín aficionado it is delicious.

FISH AND SEAFOOD

The Spanish eat the most fish and shellfish per capita of any nation on earth except for the Japanese. All over Spain there are fantastic fish restaurants and fishmongers serving nothing but the freshest fish, but strange as it may seem, the Spanish source a lot of their seafood from the UK. Visit almost any fishing port in the British Isles and you'll find Spanish refrigerated lorries waiting to pick up their catch and hotfoot it back to Spain.

Finding really fresh fish in the UK is often difficult, however, so it is very much worthwhile building up a relationship with a good fishmonger. He will be happy to order things especially for you and advise you on what is available at any particular moment.

Sadly, overfishing and poor management have led to serious ethical issues that plague our fisheries today. At Barrafina we work with our fishmongers to source only sustainable fish and seafood. You can look for the MSC (Marine Stewardship Council) badge, which is a sign of good practice.

The Spanish cook a lot of their fish on the plancha, a flat grill that is perfectly suited to the job. We suggest that at home you invest in a really good-quality, large, heavy-bottomed, non-stick frying pan. The heavy base is necessary to provide an even heat. Make sure your fish has been properly dried before you put it into the pan, and make sure the pan is hot and well oiled. If you follow these steps the rest is easy! To test if fish is cooked through, prod it with a toothpick. If there is resistance from the fish it is not yet ready; if the toothpick slides easily through to the bone, it is done.

BABY RED MULLET WITH CELERY SALAD

More than almost any other fish we know, red mullet needs to be eaten really fresh. It seems to deteriorate much faster than other species. Make sure that the mullet you buy is in top condition by using your eyes and nose: the fish should be bright-eyed and shiny, its gills should be bright and red and it should not smell strongly of iodine, as this species does when it is stale. Once your mullet have been purchased the rest of the job is easy.

SERVES 4 AS A TAPA

4 large sticks of celery
12 fresh mint leaves, finely sliced
4 baby red mullet (about 150g each), gutted and cleaned
4 bay leaves, fresh if possible
50ml olive oil
Maldon salt
1 tablespoon Ajillo (see page 206)
100ml extra virgin olive oil
60ml fresh lemon juice

Peel the celery with a potato peeler to remove the stringy ribs and cut the stalks into 2mm half-moons. Stuff each fish with a fresh bay leaf.

Put a sauté pan or a heavy-bottomed frying pan on a medium heat. Add the olive oil and heat until almost smoking. Sprinkle a little Maldon salt into the bottom of the pan, then add the fish and cook for 2 to 3 minutes on each side. If they start to look dry, add a little more oil. Use the toothpick technique (see page 45) if necessary to see when the fish are ready, then remove them from the pan to 4 serving plates and drizzle with the ajillo.

Put the celery, mint, extra virgin olive oil and lemon juice into a serving bowl. Season with salt and pepper, mix well and serve with the mullet.

COD WITH A WARM SALAD OF LENTILS AND MOJAMA

The earthiness of the lentils really works well with the cod in this soothing, wintry dish. For a more summery version you can serve the lentils cold with a little squeeze of lemon juice. Cod stocks have been severely depleted over the years, but there are still sustainable cod fisheries out there. Look for the MSC label to guarantee the source.

SERVES 4 AS A MAIN

240g brown lentils
1 large onion, peeled and halved
8 bay leaves, fresh if possible
1 bulb of fennel, cut into quarters
a small bunch of fresh thyme, stalks tied together
100ml olive oil
4 fillets of cod (about 180–200g each), skin on
Maldon salt and freshly ground black pepper
2 large shallots, peeled and finely diced
½ a bulb of fennel, finely chopped
5 tablespoons Moscatel vinegar
20 fresh mint leaves, finely sliced
50g mojama (see page 18), very thinly sliced

Put the lentils, onion, bay leaves, quartered fennel and thyme into a large pan and add 4 litres of water. Bring to the boil, then reduce the heat to a simmer and cook for 45 minutes, or until the lentils are tender. Drain the lentils, then remove the onion, fennel, thyme and bay leaves and discard.

In a heavy-bottomed non-stick frying pan heat 50ml of olive oil until it is just beginning to smoke. Add the cod fillets to the pan, skin side down. Season with salt and pepper and cook for 5 minutes. Turn the fillets over, season again and cook for another 5 minutes, or until the fish is cooked through. Remove from the pan and leave to rest for a couple of minutes in a warm place.

While the cod is cooking, finish the lentils. Heat 25ml of olive oil in a heavy-bottomed frying pan until it is just beginning to smoke. Add the shallots and the finely chopped fennel and cook for 2 to 3 minutes over a medium heat. Do not let the vegetables colour. Add the lentils and heat through, then remove from the heat and stir in the remaining 25ml of oil and the Moscatel vinegar. Add the mint and season well with salt and pepper.

Put the lentils into a serving dish and place the cod on top, drizzling over any juices. Arrange the mojama on top of the cod and serve.

BRILL WITH GARLIC AND LEMON

Brill is often overlooked, and unwisely so, as it is a fabulous fish with wonderful white meat and a delicate flavour. When Nieves first cooked this Basque dish we were blown away by its simplicity and by the incredible effect of the Moscatel vinegar combined with the garlic. This combination can be used with other flat fish, such as turbot or plaice.

SERVES 4 AS A MAIN

10 tablespoons good-quality olive oil
400g small new potatoes, cooked and cut in half
20g unsalted butter
Maldon salt
4 brill (about150g each)
4 garlic cloves, peeled and finely sliced
3 large shallots, peeled and finely chopped
juice of 1 lemon
a small bunch of fresh flat-leaf parsley, finely chopped
3 tablespoons Moscatel vinegar

Heat 4 tablespoons of olive oil in a sauté pan or heavy-bottomed frying pan until almost smoking. Add the potatoes and the butter and cook for 4 to 5 minutes on each side.

At the same time put a non-stick sauté pan or heavy-bottomed frying pan on the heat, large enough to take the brill. Add 4 tablespoons of olive oil and sprinkle in a little Maldon salt. When the oil is almost smoking add the fish, dark skin side down first, and cook for 3 to 4 minutes on each side.

Heat 2 tablespoons of olive oil in a small pan. Add the garlic and shallots and cook gently until they start to turn golden. Add the lemon juice, half the parsley and the Moscatel vinegar and swirl the sauce around the pan until it emulsifies and starts to thicken. Pour over the potatoes, add the remaining parsley and cook for a further minute.

Arrange the brill on serving plates with the potatoes and drizzle some of the sauce over the fish.

HAKE WITH FRESH PEAS
AND CECINA

Although peas straight from the garden are unbeatable when at their best, frozen petits pois come a very fine second in the winter months and would work well here as a substitute. Frozen broad beans are not as good as fresh, but will work in this recipe if you cannot find fresh ones.

SERVES 4 AS A MAIN

5 tablespoons good-quality olive oil
Maldon salt and freshly ground black pepper
800g hake, cut into 4 x 3cm medallions
2 large shallots, peeled and finely diced
2 garlic cloves, peeled and finely chopped
200ml Chicken Stock (see page 208)
20g unsalted butter
8 fresh mint leaves, finely sliced
400g fresh peas, shelled and blanched
400g fresh broad beans, shelled and blanched
60g cecina (see page 43), finely sliced

Heat 2 tablespoons of olive oil in a heavy-bottomed non-stick frying pan over a medium heat. Sprinkle a little Maldon salt into the pan. Dry the hake with kitchen paper, add to the pan and cook for 3 minutes on each side.

Heat 2 tablespoons of olive oil in a separate pan and cook the shallots and garlic gently for 2 to 3 minutes. Add the stock and bring to the boil. (If you are using frozen peas and broad beans add them now and bring to the boil again. Reduce the heat and simmer for about 5 minutes, until the liquid has almost completely disappeared.

Add the butter, mint, and the fresh peas and broad beans. Season with salt and pepper and cook for 2 more minutes. Put the cecina into a small pan with the remaining tablespoon of olive oil and gently warm through.

Put the vegetables into a serving dish with the hake on top. Arrange the cecina over the fish and serve.

JOHN DORY WITH A FENNEL, CHICORY AND RADISH SALAD

In the summer months we like to serve delicious fresh and crunchy salads with fish cooked on the plancha. The John Dory (or San Pedro in Spanish) works very well for this. The hot fish with its crispy skin combined with the refreshing salad is delicious. We love the contrast between the two types of radish, but don't worry if you can't find the rarer black radish, just use breakfast radishes on their own. It is best to slice all the vegetables on a mandolin if you have one, as this will yield perfectly even, wafer-thin slices. If you don't have a mandolin you will need to carefully slice the vegetables by hand, as thinly as you can.

SERVES 4 AS A MAIN

FOR THE SALAD
80g black radish
16 red breakfast radishes
1 bulb of fennel
4 small heads of red chicory
8 tablespoons olive oil
4 tablespoons Moscatel vinegar
4 tablespoons chopped fresh tarragon

FOR THE FISH
50ml olive oil
Maldon salt and freshly ground black pepper
4 whole John Dory (about 400g each), heads removed, scaled and gutted but still on the bone

Using a mandolin, finely slice the radishes and the fennel. Trim the base from the chicory and discard, then separate the leaves. Set aside.

To cook the fish, heat a little olive oil in a heavy-bottomed non-stick frying pan. Sprinkle some Maldon salt into the pan, then add the fish and cook for about 5 minutes on each side, seasoning well with salt and pepper as you go and drizzling with a little extra oil if necessary.

While the fish is cooking, whisk together the olive oil and vinegar in a salad bowl. Add the radishes, fennel, red chicory and tarragon, season with salt and pepper and mix well.

When the John Dory is ready, serve it with the salad.

MACKEREL WITH GRAPES, APPLE AND AJO BLANCO

Cheap, healthy and delicious, mackerel ticks every box. We are not usually great fans of combining fruit with fish, but here it works beautifully. Mackerel is best eaten straight from the pan, so make sure you have everything else ready – ajo blanco on the plates, guests at the table – before you start cooking.

SERVES 4 AS A MAIN

1 Pink Lady apple (or other sweet apple), cored and sliced
16 seedless white grapes, halved
16 seedless red grapes, halved
2 tablespoons chopped fresh tarragon
2 tablespoons Moscatel vinegar
6 tablespoons extra virgin olive oil
Maldon salt and freshly ground black pepper
½ recipe quantity of Ajo Blanco (see page 153)
4 fillets of mackerel (about 150g each)

Put the apple, grapes, tarragon, Moscatel vinegar and 4 tablespoons of the olive oil into a bowl. Season with salt and pepper and mix well, then set aside.

Take 4 serving plates and spoon a decent dollop of ajo blanco on to each one.

Heat a heavy-bottomed non-stick frying pan until very hot and add the remaining 2 tablespoons of olive oil. Add the mackerel, skin side down, and season with salt and pepper. After 2 to 3 minutes, turn the fish, cook for 1 minute more, then remove from the pan on to kitchen paper.

Place the fish on the plates, on top of the ajo blanco. Spoon the grapes and apple over the top, with their dressing, and serve immediately.

MARINATED ANCHOVIES WITH A RED ONION, MINT AND PARSLEY SALAD

This is a slight elaboration of the classic marinated anchovy dish in that it includes piquillo peppers and is served with a little salad on the side, turning it from a simple snack into more of a starter or light meal. Don't leave the anchovies in the marinade for too long or they will 'overcook' in the vinegar. Needless to say, only perfectly fresh anchovies will do for this.

SERVES 4 AS A TAPA

500g fresh anchovies (about 25–35)
200ml olive oil
4 garlic cloves, peeled and finely sliced
a very small bunch of fresh flat-leaf parsley, chopped
4 bay leaves, fresh if possible
50ml manzanilla sherry
100ml Moscatel vinegar
150g tinned or jarred piquillo peppers (see page 18), drained and finely sliced

FOR THE SALAD
3 tablespoons extra virgin olive oil
1 tablespoon sherry vinegar
Maldon salt and freshly ground black pepper
½ a red onion, peeled and sliced into very thin half-moons
a small bunch of fresh mint, leaves picked
a small bunch of fresh flat-leaf parsley, leaves picked
1 chicory frisée, yellow tips only

Gut and butterfly the anchovies, leaving the tips of the tails intact so that the 2 fillets stay attached to each other.

Put the olive oil, garlic, parsley, bay leaves, sherry and Moscatel vinegar into a large bowl and mix well. Carefully add the anchovies to the marinade, making sure they are totally covered, and refrigerate for 2 hours.

Remove the anchovies from the marinade and arrange on a large plate. Pour the marinade through a fine sieve on top of the anchovies. Season well with salt and pepper and sprinkle the piquillo peppers over the top.

To make the salad, whisk together the extra virgin olive oil, sherry vinegar, salt and pepper in a bowl. Add all the other salad ingredients and mix well. Serve the salad with the anchovies.

MONKFISH WITH NEW POTATOES AND SPINACH

We love using these baby monkfish tails, which are the perfect size for one person. If you can't find them you can use a larger fish, allowing about 150g each. Take care not to overcook the spinach or it will release too much water and make the dish soggy.

SERVES 4 AS A MAIN

500g new potatoes
Maldon salt and freshly ground black pepper
5 tablespoons olive oil
2 large shallots, peeled and finely chopped
4 baby monkfish tails (about 125g each), membrane removed (ask your fishmonger to do this)
1 teaspoon sweet smoked paprika
160g baby spinach
1 recipe quantity of Ajillo (see page 206)

Bring a large pan of salted water to the boil. Add the potatoes and cook until just tender, then drain, leave to cool for a few minutes, and cut each potato in half lengthways.

Heat 4 tablespoons of olive oil in a large, heavy-bottomed frying pan. Add the potatoes and cook for about 7 to 8 minutes, turning them until brown on both sides. Add the shallots and fry for another 2 minutes. Season with salt and pepper.

While the shallots are cooking, heat the remaining tablespoon of olive oil in a second heavy-bottomed frying pan until just smoking and cook the monkfish for about 4 minutes on each side, or until cooked through. Season with salt and pepper.

Add the smoked paprika and spinach to the pan of potatoes and cook for about a minute, or until the spinach is just beginning to wilt. Remove from the heat immediately and serve with the monkfish, drizzled with a little ajillo.

MONKFISH TAILS WITH SEAFOOD RICE

This is a really delicious reworking of the Spanish classic paella. Here, instead of all the ingredients being cooked together in a large paella dish, the monkfish is fried separately and served on top of the rice, which is cooked in a traditional pan. If you can't find the small monkfish tails we use at Barrafina, you can use larger monkfish fillets, cut in half.

SERVES 6–8 AS A MAIN

2 dried choricero peppers (see page 18), soaked in warm water for 2 hours
6–7 tablespoons good-quality olive oil
1 large shallot, peeled and cut in half lengthways
1 whole head of garlic, halved horizontally
1 dried red chilli
2 bay leaves, fresh if possible
1 teaspoon sweet smoked paprika
4 litres Bisque (see page 211)
320g Calasparra rice
250g palourde clams, cleaned
250g mussels, cleaned
16 large raw king prawns, shell on
Maldon salt and freshly ground pepper
1 tablespoon chopped fresh flat-leaf parsley
1 tablespoon Ajillo (see page 206)
4 baby monkfish tails (about 125g each), membrane removed (ask your fishmonger to do this)

Drain the choricero peppers, then remove the seeds and slice. Heat 2 tablespoons of oil in a very large pan over a medium heat and add the shallot and the whole head of garlic. Cook for a few minutes, until the shallots are translucent, then add the choriceros, dried red chilli, bay leaves, paprika and bisque. Bring back to a gentle simmer and cook until the liquid is reduced by half.

Heat 4 more tablespoons of oil in a large wide sauté pan or heavy-bottomed frying pan and add the rice, stirring to coat it well with the oil. Pour in the bisque mixture through a sieve, squeezing out any juices still left in the solids. Discard the solids. Stir for about 10 minutes over a medium heat. Add the clams, mussels and prawns and keep cooking until the rice is tender (about 20 minutes).

Season the rice with salt and pepper, sprinkle the parsley over the top and drizzle over the ajillo. Cover with foil and leave to rest for 5 to 10 minutes.

While the rice is resting, heat a little more oil in a heavy-bottomed frying pan and fry the monkfish tails for 8 to 10 minutes, until cooked through, turning a few times and seasoning with salt and pepper as you go. Uncover the rice, arrange the monkfish on top, and serve.

PAN-FRIED WHOLE SEA BREAM

A bream straight from the sea is a wonderful thing, but farmed sea bass is an excellent substitute, extremely fresh and normally available all year round. This is a great dish to cook on a well-oiled barbecue – but be careful not to let the skin stick and only start to cook the fish when the flames have died down and just the embers remain.

SERVES 4 AS A MAIN

2 whole sea bream, scaled and gutted
8 bay leaves, fresh if possible
a bunch of fresh thyme
1 lemon
50ml good-quality olive oil
Maldon salt and freshly ground black pepper
4 dessertspoons Ajillo (see page 206)

Stuff the cavity of each fish with half the bay leaves and thyme and squeeze in the juice of the lemon.

Heat 2 dessertspoons of olive oil in a large non-stick sauté pan or heavy-bottomed frying pan over a medium heat. Place the fish in the pan and season with salt and pepper. Cook for 6 to 7 minutes, then carefully turn the fish over with a spatula, adding more olive oil if necessary. Cook for a further 6 to 7 minutes, testing with a toothpick (see page 45) to see whether the fish is cooked.

Drizzle with ajillo and serve.

SEA BASS WITH PIQUILLO SAUCE AND JERUSALEM ARTICHOKES

We love the vibrant colour, flavour and textural combinations in this Anglo-Spanish fusion dish. Wild sea bass is much superior to the farmed variety and should be sought out where possible. Dry the fish thoroughly with kitchen paper before cooking, to help prevent it sticking to the pan.

SERVES 4 AS A MAIN

300g Jerusalem artichokes
Maldon salt and freshly ground black pepper
125ml olive oil
2 large shallots, peeled and diced
1½ garlic cloves, peeled and finely chopped
2 bay leaves, fresh if possible
1 x 390g tin or jar of piquillo peppers (see page 18), drained
1 tablespoon caster sugar
50ml manzanilla sherry
12 fresh sage leaves
4 fillets of wild sea bass (about 180–200g each)

Peel the Jerusalem artichokes and cook in plenty of salted boiling water until tender – about 30 minutes. Drain, allow to cool, then cut in half lengthways and set aside.

Heat 25ml of the oil in a medium-sized pan. Add the shallots, garlic and bay leaves and gently fry for about 5 minutes, until just translucent. Finely slice the piquillo peppers and add to the pan with the caster sugar. Stir well. Add the manzanilla and 125ml of water, bring to the boil, then reduce the heat to a simmer and cook for another 5 minutes. Remove from the heat and allow to cool a little. Put into a blender or food processor and blitz until smooth. Season with salt and pepper and set aside.

Heat 75ml of olive oil in a heavy-bottomed frying pan and brown the Jerusalem artichokes on all sides. Add the sage leaves and season well.

While the artichokes are browning, score the skin of the sea bass every 0.5cm or so, taking care not to score all the way to the edge of the fish. Heat the remaining 25ml of oil in a large, heavy-bottomed, non-stick frying pan until smoking and fry the sea bass, skin side down, for about 6 minutes. Season well, then carefully turn the fish and fry on the other side for another 2 minutes, seasoning again.

Serve the fish as soon as it is ready, with the piquillo sauce and Jerusalem artichokes.

SKATE WITH BLACK OLIVES, PINENUTS AND ANCHOVIES

Skate is one of our favourite fish, and with this robust accompaniment it is really shown at its best. Skate can stick quite easily, so a good-quality, heavy-bottomed, non-stick frying pan is a worthwhile investment for the skate aficionado.

SERVES 4 AS A MAIN

50g pinenuts
250g Aragón olives, pitted
50g salted anchovies
1 garlic clove, peeled
100ml olive oil
25ml Moscatel vinegar
8 fresh mint leaves, sliced lengthways
½ a large shallot, peeled and finely diced
60ml extra virgin olive oil
4 pieces of skate (about 250g each)
Maldon salt and freshly ground black pepper

Preheat the oven to 180°C/350°F/gas 4. Put the pinenuts on a baking tray and roast in the oven for 2 to 3 minutes, until lightly browned. Remove from the oven and set aside.

Put the olives, anchovies, garlic, 75ml of olive oil and 15ml of Moscatel vinegar into a food processor and blitz until smooth.

In a small bowl mix together the roasted pinenuts, mint, shallot, the remaining 10ml of Moscatel vinegar and the extra virgin olive oil. Set aside.

Heat 25ml of olive oil in a large, heavy-bottomed, non-stick frying pan until just smoking. Carefully pat the skate dry with kitchen paper and cook in the hot oil for 5 minutes on the thin side. Season well. Turn the fish over to its thicker side and cook for another 8 minutes. Drizzle with a little more olive oil if needed.

Spoon a good dollop of the olive paste on to each serving plate. Put the fish on top, and spoon another dollop of paste over the upper side. Serve with the pinenut salad.

TUNA IN ESCABECHE

Originally a Persian 'sweet and sour' treatment for meat, this technique was brought to Spain by the Moors. Use best-quality sustainable yellowfin tuna and remember not to overcook it. The fish needs only to be seared, leaving the middle raw. If you don't use all the parsley oil, it will keep in the fridge for a couple of days.

SERVES 4 AS A TAPA OR LIGHT LUNCH

FOR THE TUNA
20ml olive oil
4 best-quality tuna steaks,
3cm thick (about 150g each)
1 x 390g tin or jar of piquillo peppers (see page 18), drained and cut into thin strips
30ml extra virgin olive oil
3 tablespoons chopped fresh chives

FOR THE PARSLEY OIL
a large bunch of fresh flat-leaf parsley, thick stalks removed
200ml extra virgin olive oil
1 garlic clove, peeled and finely chopped
Maldon salt and freshly ground black pepper

FOR THE ESCABECHE
200ml extra virgin olive oil
150ml Moscatel vinegar
3 garlic cloves, peeled and crushed
3 bay leaves, fresh if possible

To make the parsley oil, bring a pan of water to the boil. Immerse the parsley in the water for 30 seconds, then remove it and plunge it into iced water. Drain and dry on kitchen paper. Put the oil into a blender or food processor with the parsley and garlic, and blitz. Season with salt and pepper to taste and set aside.

For the escabeche, place the oil, Moscatel vinegar, garlic and bay leaves in a pan and bring to a gentle simmer. Immediately remove from the heat and set aside to cool.

Heat the 20ml of olive oil in a large sauté pan or heavy-bottomed frying pan and sprinkle in a little salt. When the oil is almost smoking, cook the tuna for 1½ minutes each side. It should still be pink in the middle. Remove from the heat and set aside. When the escabeche has cooled, add the tuna steaks and leave for 10 minutes.

Put the piquillo peppers into a small bowl and add 30ml of extra virgin olive oil and the chives.

Spoon a little parsley oil and some of the piquillo peppers on to each serving plate. Take the tuna out of the escabeche and lay it on top. Spoon over a little of the escabeche, then put the remaining piquillo peppers on top of the tuna and finish with a drizzle of extra virgin olive oil.

TUNA TARTARE

Although perhaps not entirely Spanish in its make-up, when Nieves first produced this dish we all knew we were on to a winner. The combination of these glistening cubes with the silky smooth guacamole and Oriental seasoning is our favourite way to eat the fish. We are normally very much averse to using chef's rings for presenting food, but in this case it seems to make sense. However, don't worry if you don't possess one of these things, as you can just spoon the tuna on to the plate.

SERVES 4 AS A TAPA

a small bunch of fresh coriander
2 ripe avocados, peeled, stoned and roughly chopped
1 garlic clove, peeled
Maldon salt and freshly ground black pepper
75ml olive oil
juice of ½ a lemon
juice of 1½ limes
400g loin of tuna, in one piece
20g sesame seeds
50ml sesame oil
40ml light soy sauce

Set aside 4 sprigs of coriander to use as a garnish, and place the rest of the bunch into a blender or food processor with the avocados, garlic, salt, pepper, 50ml of the olive oil and a little of the lemon and lime juice. Blitz until you have a smooth mousse. Taste it and add more lemon and lime juice until you like the flavour and consistency.

Trim any discoloured bits from the outside of the tuna. With a very sharp knife, cut the tuna into 0.5cm slices, then into 0.5cm long strips and finally into 0.5cm cubes.

Put the sesame seeds, sesame oil, soy sauce and the remaining olive oil into a bowl. Add the tuna and mix well.

To serve, place a 6cm ring mould on a serving plate. Spoon a quarter of the tuna into the ring, smoothing the top to make a gentle cone. Carefully remove the ring and spoon a good-sized quenelle of guacamole mousse alongside the tuna. Place a little sprig of coriander on top of the tuna and repeat for the remaining plates.

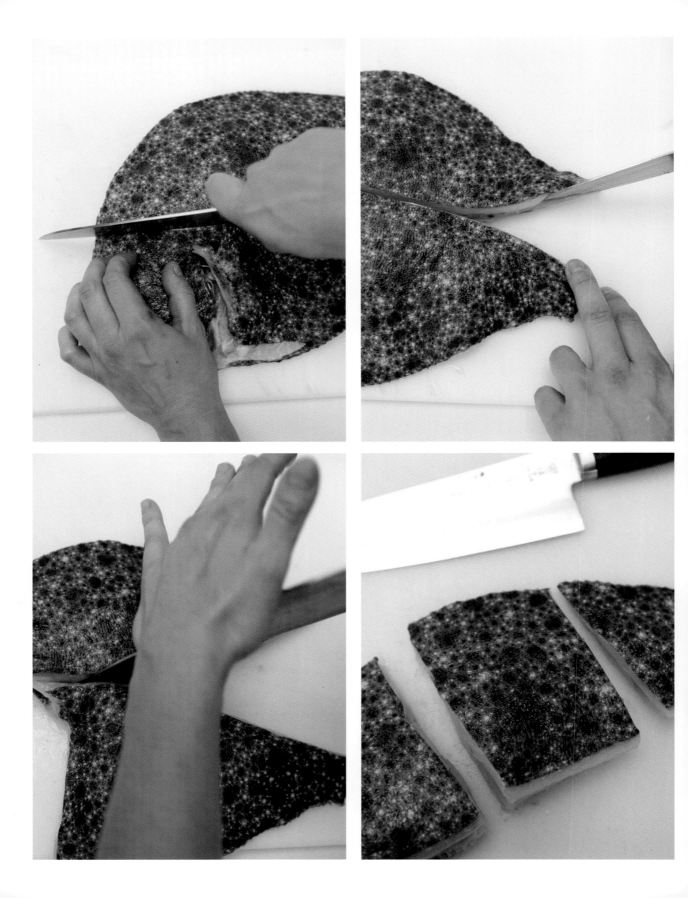

TURBOT WITH CAVOLO NERO

A great friend and famous food writer came into the restaurant one day for lunch and ordered the turbot. When the fish arrived he exclaimed in horror, 'But . . . you have given me the tail end!' So that your guests should not be thus offended, we suggest you ask your fishmonger for the thicker, middle part of the fish that is more highly regarded. Here we serve it with cavolo nero, a dark Italian brassica, but spring greens would also work well.

SERVES 4 AS A MAIN

Maldon salt and freshly ground black pepper
400g cavolo nero
4 tablespoons good-quality olive oil
4 large shallots, peeled and finely diced
4 garlic cloves, peeled and finely sliced
12 bay leaves, fresh if possible
200ml manzanilla or fino sherry
200ml cooking brandy
250ml Bisque (see page 211)
250ml double cream
4 medallions of turbot (150–175g each)

Bring a large pan of salted water to the boil. Add the cavolo nero and blanch for 2 to 3 minutes, then drain it and plunge it into iced water.

Heat 2 tablespoons of olive oil in a sauté pan or heavy-bottomed frying pan over a medium heat. Add the shallots, garlic and bay leaves and cook gently for 3 to 4 minutes without allowing them to colour. Add the sherry and brandy, bring back to the boil and simmer for 6 to 7 minutes.

Add the bisque, bring back to the boil, and cook over a high heat for 5 minutes. Add the cream, lower the heat and simmer until the quantity is reduced by half – about 7 minutes. Add the cavolo nero and simmer very gently over a low heat until warmed through. Season with salt and pepper to taste, then cover the pan and keep warm.

Heat the remaining 2 tablespoons of olive oil in a heavy-bottomed non-stick frying pan over a medium heat and sprinkle in some Maldon salt. When the oil is almost smoking, add the turbot, dark skin side down, and cook for 4 to 5 minutes. Turn the fish over and cook for a further 4 to 5 minutes.

To serve, spoon the cavolo nero on to serving plates and top with the turbot.

FRITURA

The Spanish are experts at deep-frying fish. The special flour, combined with really fresh fish and hot, clean oil, is an irresistible combination. You can mix and match almost any sort of seafood for this dish as long as the quality is good. If you have a small deep-fryer you may have to fry the fish in batches.

SERVES 4–6 AS A TAPA

1 litre oil for deep-frying
a handful of fresh flat-leaf parsley, leaves picked
Maldon salt and freshly ground black pepper
2 lemons
150g special flour for frying (see page 17)
250g baby monkfish, cut into 35g cubes
400–500g brill or turbot, cut into 50g pieces
200g large king prawns, shell on
250g squid, cleaned and cut into 1cm rings (about 400g before cleaning)

Heat the oil to 180°C in a deep-fryer or a large deep pan. Fry the parsley leaves for 30 seconds, being careful to avoid spitting oil, then remove them with a slotted spoon on to kitchen paper. Season with salt and pepper and keep to one side.

Cut one of the lemons into 1cm slices and the other into 4 to 6 wedges. Put the flour into a large mixing bowl and add the fish, prawns, squid and lemon slices. Mix well to coat the fish and lemon with the flour, then dust off any excess.

When frying the fish, start with the ones that take longest. First add the monkfish to the hot oil, one piece at a time, and fry for 45 seconds. Next, add the brill or turbot and fry for a further 20 seconds.

Add the prawns and fry for 20 seconds, then the squid and fry for a further 20 seconds. Finally add the lemon slices and fry for a further 45 seconds.

Remove everything from the oil piece by piece and place directly on to kitchen paper. Season with salt and pepper, scatter over the fried parsley and serve immediately, with the lemon wedges.

SQUID STUFFED WITH CEPS AND PRAWNS

We were always extremely suspicious of stuffed squid until Nieves produced this mind-changing example. All too often (away from our home stoves) we had tried variations where the dish was dry and neither the squid benefited from the filling nor vice versa. Here, the cep and prawn mix stays moist and accompanies the flavour of the squid brilliantly.

SERVES 4 AS A TAPA OR LIGHT LUNCH

250ml Bisque (see page 211)
6 tablespoons olive oil
350g fresh ceps/porcini mushrooms, roughly chopped
1 large shallot, peeled and finely diced
1 garlic clove, peeled and finely chopped
300g raw peeled king prawns, roughly chopped
4 medium squid, cleaned
Maldon salt and freshly ground black pepper
4 tablespoons finely chopped chives
juice of 1 lemon
a handful of fresh flat-leaf parsley, chopped

Put the bisque into a small, heavy-bottomed pan over a medium heat and bring to the boil, then simmer until reduced and thick – there should be about 4 tablespoons left. Set aside to keep warm.

Heat 2 tablespoons of olive oil in a heavy-bottomed frying pan until just smoking. Add the mushrooms over a medium to high heat and cook until they are nicely browned. Add the shallots and garlic and fry for another 2 minutes.

Add the prawns and the squid tentacles and 2 more tablespoons of oil and cook for 5 minutes. Season well with salt and pepper. Add the chives and lemon juice and cook for a further 2 minutes.

Remove from the heat and set aside until cool, then carefully spoon the stuffing into the squid bodies, securing them with wooden toothpicks. Don't be tempted to overfill the squid or the stuffing will fall out during cooking.

Heat the remaining oil in a large, heavy-bottomed frying pan and fry the squid for about 2 to 3 minutes on each side, seasoning them with salt and pepper as you go.

Serve the squid with a spoonful of the sauce over the top and a scattering of chopped parsley.

SQUID WRAPPED IN PANCETTA WITH INK SAUCE

Whenever we serve this as a special in Barrafina it vanishes almost immediately. The smokiness of the pancetta is offset by the nutty squid, and the dark unctuousness of the ink sauce is difficult to resist. You can also use small cuttlefish for this recipe.

SERVES 4 AS A TAPA

1kg small squid, cleaned
(about 400g after cleaning)
8–12 thin slices of smoked pancetta
100ml olive oil
salt and freshly ground black pepper
4 tablespoons Squid Ink Sauce
(see page 212)
1 dessertspoon Ajillo (see page 206)

First prepare the squid. With a very sharp knife make a cut down the length of each squid body, cutting through the top layer of the tube but not the bottom. Open the bodies up to lay them flat. Score the skin of the squid every 2mm from top to bottom, taking care not to cut right through.

Lay a piece of pancetta flat on your chopping board. Roll one squid body up lengthways like a large cigar, then place it on top of the pancetta and roll that around the middle of the squid a couple of times. Leave to rest, with the ends of the pancetta underneath the body of the squid to keep them together.

Heat the olive oil in a large, heavy-bottomed frying pan until just beginning to smoke. Add the squid and fry gently until nicely browned on all sides and cooked through, seasoning well with salt and pepper as you go.

Heat the ink sauce in a small pan and spoon a good dollop on to each serving plate. Lay your squid on top, with a little ajillo drizzled over.

CUTTLEFISH WITH RUNNER BEANS AND CHICKPEAS

We Love Cuttlefish! It is much less admired in the UK than its cousin the squid, but it has a wonderful nuttiness to it which squid does not. We try to buy small cuttlefish, which are often more tender than the larger of the species. When Nieves first put this dish on as a special at Barrafina it was sold out before we could try it. We always consider this a very good sign!

SERVES 4 AS A MAIN

300g runner (or French) beans, topped and tailed
400g cuttlefish or squid, cleaned and cut into 0.5cm rings
1 tablespoon cumin seeds
1 tablespoon sweet smoked paprika
2 garlic cloves, peeled and finely chopped
½ teaspoon cayenne pepper
a small bunch of fresh thyme
6 bay leaves, fresh if possible
15 tablespoons extra virgin olive oil
240g dried chickpeas, soaked in cold water overnight and drained
1 large shallot, peeled and finely chopped
Maldon salt and freshly ground black pepper
500ml Bisque (see page 211)
4 tablespoons finely chopped fresh flat-leaf parsley

If using runner beans, slice them on the diagonal, about 1cm wide. If using French beans, cut them into 2cm lengths.

Put the cuttlefish into a bowl. Add cumin seeds, smoked paprika, garlic, cayenne, thyme, 3 of the bay leaves and 1 tablespoon of olive oil, and leave to marinate in the fridge for at least 2 hours and preferably overnight.

Put the drained chickpeas into a large pan of cold water and add the shallots and the remaining 3 bay leaves. Bring to the boil over a medium heat, then cook for 45 minutes, until the chickpeas are tender. Drain and set aside.

Bring a large pan of salted water to the boil. Add the beans and blanch for 2 minutes, then plunge them into cold water. Drain and set aside.

Heat 8 tablespoons of olive oil in a large sauté pan or heavy-bottomed frying pan over a medium heat. Remove the cuttlefish from the marinade, discarding the herbs and garlic, and add to the pan. Cook gently for 5 minutes, then add another 4 tablespoons of olive oil and stir well.

Add the bisque, bring to the boil, then reduce the heat and simmer until reduced by half. Season with salt and pepper, then add the beans and cooked chickpeas and cook for 2 minutes.

Add the parsley and serve with a drizzle of olive oil.

DIVER-CAUGHT SCALLOPS WITH JERUSALEM ARTICHOKE AND JAMÓN PURÉE

The combination of scallops with the artichoke and jamón purée is a magical one. We often discuss whether to eat the orange scallop roes. Much argument follows, the result of which is that at home we do but in the restaurant we don't. You must do as you please.

SERVES 4 AS A TAPA

½ recipe quantity of Jerusalem Artichoke and Jamón Purée (see page 215)
50ml olive oil
8 large diver-caught scallops, cleaned and prepared
Maldon salt and freshly ground black pepper
1 red chilli, seeded and finely sliced
2 sprigs of fresh flat-leaf parsley, leaves finely sliced

Put the artichoke and jamón purée into a small pan and heat gently. Set aside.

Heat the oil in a heavy-bottomed frying pan until smoking. Add the scallops and fry for 2 minutes on each side or until cooked, seasoning well with salt and pepper.

Spoon a little of the purée on to each serving plate, and sit the scallops proudly on top, sprinkled with the chilli and parsley.

QUEEN SCALLOP EMPANADILLAS WITH RED ONION AND MINT SALAD

We first had these cooked for us while dining with some percebes fishermen and their families in the small town of La Guardia, on the Portuguese border of Galicia.

SERVES 8 AS A TAPA OR 4 AS A MAIN

FOR THE EMPANADILLAS
100ml olive oil, plus 2 tablespoons
3 garlic cloves, peeled and finely chopped
2 courgettes, cut into 0.5cm dice
1 aubergine, cut into 0.5cm dice
Maldon salt and freshly ground black pepper
3 bay leaves, fresh if possible
1 teaspoon smoked paprika
1 teaspoon cayenne pepper
500ml tomate frito (see page 18) or passata
350g queen scallops
500g puff pastry, defrosted if frozen
1 free-range egg
1 tablespoon water
plain flour for dusting

FOR THE SALAD
1 large red onion, peeled and finely sliced
a handful of fresh mint leaves
1 small shallot, peeled and finely chopped
1 tablespoon extra virgin olive oil
1 tablespoon Pedro Ximénez balsamic vinegar

Heat the 100ml of olive oil in a large sauté pan or large, heavy-bottomed frying pan and cook the garlic gently for 1 to 2 minutes, without allowing it to colour. Add the courgettes and aubergine, season with salt and pepper, then add the bay leaves, paprika and cayenne and cook gently for 35 to 40 minutes, stirring occasionally. Add the tomate frito and cook for 5 minutes more.

Heat 2 tablespoons of olive oil in a separate heavy-bottomed frying pan and sear the scallops for 3 to 4 minutes. Season with salt and pepper and add to the aubergines and courgettes. Simmer for 3 to 4 minutes, then remove from the heat and leave to cool.

Preheat the oven to 180°C/350°F/gas 4. On a floured surface roll out one-third of the pastry into a rectangle 2mm thick. Using an 11–12cm pastry cutter, cut out discs and set aside on floured baking parchment. Repeat this process using the rest of the pastry until you have cut out as many discs as you can.

When the scallop mixture is cool, beat the egg and water in a small bowl. On a floured surface, lay out the puff pastry discs and spoon 1½ tablespoons of the scallop mix into the middle of each one. Fold the discs over to create half-moon parcels and crimp the edge gently with a fork. Brush the parcels with the egg wash and place them on a tray lined with baking parchment. Bake for 12 to 15 minutes, until golden brown.

While the empanadillas are baking, combine all the salad ingredients in a bowl and season with salt and pepper. Serve with the empanadillas.

SCALLOP CARPACCIO

This dish is best made when you've happened to stumble across brilliantly fresh scallops rather than being planned too far ahead, as it relies almost entirely on the freshness of the scallops. Use your very finest extra virgin olive oil, as this is the only other major factor in the success of the dish.

SERVES 4 AS A TAPA

4 large and extremely fresh diver-caught scallops, cleaned and sliced into super-thin rounds (about 2mm)
8 dessertspoons extra virgin olive oil
4 dessertspoons lemon juice
a pinch of salt
1 teaspoon sesame oil
1 teaspoon chopped fresh chives
a couple of sprigs of fresh coriander
baby salad leaves (optional)

Gently lay the scallop slices on a flat plate.

Combine the olive oil, lemon juice, salt, sesame oil and chopped chives in a small bowl and mix well.

Carefully spoon the dressing over the scallops and serve immediately, garnished with the coriander and the baby salad leaves.

Sultanas

Sauce

alad

alad

rt

of Spanish Cheeses

narrafu

CLANS A LA PLANCHA

This is so simple that it is essential all the ingredients are really prime. Removing the clams to a bowl with the dressing the moment they open prevents them overcooking. Strangely, the clams seem to release most of their juice after they have opened and are in the bowl, so you preserve this as well.

SERVES 4 AS A TAPA

100ml extra virgin olive oil
3–4 dessertspoons good-quality olive oil
1kg palourde clams, cleaned
2 lemons
2 tablespoons Ajillo (see page 206)
Maldon salt and freshly ground black pepper
1 tablespoon chopped fresh flat-leaf parsley

Heat the extra virgin olive oil in a pan until warm, not hot, then take it off the heat. Heat 3 dessertspoons of good-quality olive oil in a large sauté pan or heavy-bottomed frying pan over a medium heat and add the clams, discarding any that are not tightly shut or that refuse to shut when you tap them. Remove them one by one as they open and place them in the pan containing the warm oil. Add a little more olive oil to the clams in the sauté pan if necessary to help them open. If any remain shut, discard them.

Cut the lemons in half and squeeze the juice through a small sieve over the open clams. Add the ajillo and season with salt and pepper. Sprinkle with parsley, mix well and serve.

RAZOR CLAMS WITH BROAD BEANS AND JAMÓN

Razor clams are usually on the menu at Barrafina. They have had a bit of a resurgence recently, and it is great to see them around and about on other London menus. Make sure the clams are alive when you buy them. You can check this by poking one on the nose with your finger and seeing if it moves. If you can't get fresh broad beans you can use frozen, but the results will not be as good.

SERVES 4 AS A TAPA

Maldon salt and freshly ground black pepper
1kg fresh broad beans (weight before shelling), shelled and peeled
8 tablespoons extra virgin olive oil
20g Ibérico or Serrano ham, cut into strips
2 large shallots, peeled and finely chopped
2 garlic cloves, peeled and finely chopped
200ml Chicken Stock (see page 208)
20 small razor clams, cleaned
75ml good-quality olive oil
2 tablespoons Ajillo (see page 206)

Bring a large pan of well-salted water to the boil. Add the beans and blanch them for 1 minute, then drain them and plunge them into iced water for 2 minutes. Drain the beans and pat dry.

Heat 4 tablespoons of extra virgin olive oil in a large sauté pan or heavy-bottomed frying pan over a medium heat. Add the ham and cook gently for 30 seconds. Add the shallots and cook for a further 30 seconds, then add the garlic and cook for a couple of seconds more. Add another 4 tablespoons of oil and the stock, and simmer until the liquid has reduced by half. Add the broad beans, season with salt and pepper and cook for 1 minute more.

In a separate sauté pan or heavy-bottomed frying pan, heat the olive oil until smoking. Add the razor clams, turning them flesh side down as soon as they open and discarding any that don't. Cook for 1 minute, until the flesh is golden brown.

Divide the clams between serving plates and spoon the broad beans and ham over the top and into the shells. Drizzle with the ajillo and serve.

MUSSELS WITH SHERRY VINAIGRETTE

This way of serving mussels is extremely common throughout northern Spain. You can eat the mussels hot or cold, so any leftovers can be stored in the fridge for another time.

SERVES 4 AS A TAPA

150ml extra virgin olive oil
50ml sherry vinegar
4 tablespoons chopped fresh chives
½ a green pepper, seeded and extra finely diced
½ a red pepper, seeded and extra finely diced
1 small onion, peeled and extra finely diced
Maldon salt and freshly ground black pepper
1kg best-quality fresh mussels, cleaned

Put 100ml of the extra virgin olive oil into a large pan with the sherry vinegar and chives and heat gently. Add the diced peppers and onion and season with salt and pepper.

Heat the remaining extra virgin olive oil in a sauté pan or heavy-bottomed frying pan over a medium heat. Add the mussels, discarding any that are not closed or that do not close when you tap them. Remove them with tongs as they open and put them into the pan with the sherry vinaigrette. Discard any mussels that remain closed.

Once all the mussels are cooked, stir them well into the vinaigrette and serve.

MUSSELS IN SPICY TOMATO SAUCE

At Barrafina we use deepwater mussels from the Dorset coast, which are by far the best we have ever tried. Lightly cooked in this piquant sauce they make a delicious starter, or, with lots of good bread and a little salad, a more substantial meal.

SERVES 4 AS A TAPA

6 tablespoons olive oil
1 large onion, peeled and diced
1 tablespoon fresh thyme leaves
Maldon salt and freshly ground black pepper
500ml tomate frito (see page 18) or passata
1 teaspoon cayenne pepper
1 teaspoon hot smoked paprika
600g mussels, cleaned
4 tablespoons manzanilla sherry
4 tablespoons chopped fresh flat-leaf parsley

Heat 2 tablespoons of olive oil in a small, heavy-bottomed frying pan. Add the onions and thyme and cook gently for about 10 minutes, until the onions are translucent. Season with salt and pepper and set aside.

Put the tomate frito into a medium pan and heat gently until it comes to the boil. Add the cayenne pepper and paprika, season with salt and pepper and set aside.

Heat the remaining olive oil in a large, heavy-bottomed pan until it is smoking. Throw in the mussels, discarding any that are not tightly shut or that refuse to close when you tap them. Cook for 30 seconds, then add the sherry, cover the pan, and cook until the mussels have opened. Discard any that remain shut. Add the tomato sauce and cook over a high heat for another minute to thicken the sauce.

Put the mussels and sauce into a serving dish, spoon over the onions and the chopped parsley and serve with good bread.

GRILLED LOBSTER

Lobster cooked on the plancha is very fine indeed. It is another of those ingredients which although common throughout Spain actually originate in the UK. Lobsters deteriorate quite fast once killed, so if you can face it, it is best if you can dispatch them yourself. To do this, first press the tip of a large, sharp, heavy knife into the middle of the back of the head of the lobster, then, in one clean movement, chop it in half. If you're squeamish, ask your fishmonger to do this for you.

SERVES 4 AS A TAPA OR 2 AS A MAIN

2 x 400–500g lobsters, live if possible
juice of ½ a lemon
240ml Bisque (see page 211)
180ml extra virgin olive oil
Maldon salt and freshly
ground black pepper
4 large plum tomatoes,
cut into 0.5cm cubes
4 tablespoons small fresh basil leaves
30ml Pedro Ximénez balsamic vinegar
1 large shallot, peeled and finely chopped
2 tablespoons Ajillo (see page 206)

Cut the lobsters in half lengthways with a large sharp knife and remove the claws. Spoon the brown meat out of the shell with a teaspoon and put it into a mixing bowl. Add the lemon juice and set aside for 2 to 3 minutes.

Pour the bisque into a pan over a medium heat and bring to the boil. Add the brown meat and lemon juice, then reduce the heat a little and simmer until the liquid has reduced by half.

Heat 60ml of extra virgin olive oil in a large sauté pan or heavy-bottomed frying pan over a medium heat. Add the lobster claws and cook for 3 to 4 minutes on each side, seasoning as you go. Pour in another 60ml of oil, then add the lobster bodies, flesh side down. Cook for 3 minutes, then remove the smaller claws and set aside. Turn the lobster bodies over, season with salt and pepper and cook for 5 minutes more.

Put the tomatoes and basil into a mixing bowl and add the balsamic vinegar and the remaining 60ml of extra virgin olive oil. Season with salt and pepper to taste, and add the shallots and ajillo.

Remove the lobster from the pan and divide between serving plates. Season the brown meat with salt and pepper to taste and spoon this mixture back into the head cavity. Spoon the tomato and basil dressing over the white meat, and serve.

CRAB ON TOAST

Similar to the Basque dish txangurro, this makes an excellent light lunch at home. Alternatively you can take it on a picnic, with the crab mix in a bowl and the toast wrapped separately. You can buy picked crab in all good fishmongers, but cooking and picking the crab yourself will always yield better results and will also be considerably cheaper. Just buy a large, live crab and cook it in boiling salted water for about 25 minutes. Leave to cool before picking the meat.

SERVES 4 AS A TAPA

FOR THE CRAB
7 dessertspoons olive oil
2 leeks, finely diced
4 shallots, peeled and very finely diced
3 bay leaves, fresh if possible
3 garlic cloves
100ml Bisque (see page 211)
½ teaspoon cayenne pepper
2 dessertspoons tomato purée
250g white crabmeat
125g brown crabmeat
Maldon salt and freshly ground black pepper
4 thick slices of white sourdough bread

FOR THE SALAD
2 heads of red chicory
7 breakfast radishes
1 bulb of fennel
1 Pink Lady apple (or other sweet apple), cored
8 dessertspoons extra virgin olive oil
4 dessertspoons Moscatel vinegar
1 dessertspoon finely chopped tarragon

Heat the olive oil in a large, heavy-bottomed frying pan. Add the leeks, shallots, bay leaves and 2 of the garlic cloves, peeled and sliced lengthways. Fry until the vegetables are translucent – about 7 minutes. Add the bisque, cayenne and tomato purée, bring to the boil, then reduce the heat and simmer until reduced by two-thirds.

Once the bisque has reduced, stir in all the crabmeat, season well with salt and pepper and cook for 2 more minutes. Remove from the heat, transfer to a bowl and leave to cool to room temperature. Cover with clingfilm and put into the fridge for 2 to 3 hours.

To prepare the salad, trim the base from the chicory and discard, then separate the leaves. Slice the radishes lengthways on a mandolin (or slice evenly with a knife). Put them into a large bowl. Very finely slice the fennel and finely slice the apple into half-moons. Add these to the bowl.

In a smaller bowl, whisk together the olive oil, vinegar, tarragon and a little salt and pepper to make a dressing.

When you are ready to serve, lightly toast the bread. Rub the upper side of the toast with the remaining garlic clove, cut in half, then spoon the crab mixture evenly over the toast. Toss the salad with the dressing and serve with the crab toasts.

LANGOUSTINES WITH TOMATO AND BASIL

Langoustines, or Dublin Bay prawns, deteriorate very quickly once they are dead, so you should really try to buy them alive where possible. They are extremely popular in Spain, though in fact 95 per cent of those that you see there will have come from the UK. Unlike prawns, we can confidently say that we can find better langoustines here in good old Blighty.

SERVES 4 AS A TAPA

200ml Bisque (see page 211)
4 ripe medium tomatoes, cut into 1cm cubes
2 large shallots, peeled and finely diced
5 large fresh basil leaves, cut into thin strips
4 tablespoons Pedro Ximénez balsamic vinegar
Maldon salt and freshly ground black pepper
24 raw fresh langoustines (preferably live) or large king prawns, shell on
2 tablespoons olive oil
1 tablespoon Ajillo (see page 206)

Put the bisque into a pan and bring gently to the boil. Lower the heat and simmer until reduced by three-quarters – the bisque should be thick enough to coat the back of a spoon. Leave to cool for 10 minutes.

Transfer the bisque to a mixing bowl. Add the tomatoes, shallots, basil and Pedro Ximénez balsamic vinegar, season with salt and pepper and mix well.

Cut the langoustines in half lengthways down the back of the head. Heat the olive oil in a large griddle pan over a medium heat, and when it is almost smoking, add the langoustines flesh side down and cook for 1 minute. You may need to do this in batches.

Serve the langoustines with the tomato salad scattered over the top, and finish with a little drizzle of ajillo.

PRAWNS A LA SAL

Spain has some of the finest prawns in the world, with many wonderful local species being supremely regarded. Huge, bright red carabinieros, delicately flavoured langostinos de San Luca, and the famous red prawns of Palamos all have near-mythical status in Spanish seafood restaurants. In Mallorca our favourites are the excellent gambas de Soller. Cooking in salt really brings out the flavour of these great prawns, which sadly are hard to come by in the UK. Whichever prawns you use, make sure they are really fresh.

SERVES 4 AS A TAPA

400g table salt
4 very large prawns, shell on
(about 75–80g each)

Heat half the salt in a large, heavy-bottomed pan. Lay the prawns on top and pour the rest of the salt on top of them. Cook over a medium to high heat for 10 minutes, then turn the prawns over and cook for another 3 minutes.

Remove the prawns from the pan and chip off any salt still adhering to them. Serve immediately.

BARRAFINA SEAFOOD SOUP

A really good seafood soup is one of those special occasion dishes that sets the mood for a five-star party. This is quite a reduced soup and ends up almost like grilled seafood with a soupy sauce. Make sure your diners are provided with sufficient crackers and picks and bowls for discarding shells.

SERVES 4 AS A MAIN

275ml extra virgin olive oil
2 garlic cloves, peeled and finely sliced, plus 1 whole clove, peeled
1 carrot, peeled and cut into 1cm dice
3 bay leaves, fresh if possible
1 large shallot, peeled and finely chopped
1 leek (white part only), cut into 1cm dice
1 fennel bulb, cut into 1cm dice
2 sticks of celery, cut into 1 cm dice
1 large white potato, peeled and cut into 1cm dice
80ml passata
15ml brandy
15ml Pernod
1 litre Bisque (see page 211)
1 star anise
4 tablespoons Ajillo (see page 206)
2 lobsters (400–500g each), cut in half lengthways, bodies and claws separated
Maldon salt and freshly ground black pepper
400g monkfish, off the bone, cut into 2.5cm cubes
250g cleaned squid, with tentacles, bodies cut into 1cm rings

Heat 2 tablespoons of olive oil in a large pan over a medium heat. Add the sliced garlic and cook gently for 2 minutes, then add the carrot and bay leaves and cook for a further 2 minutes.

Add the shallot, leek, fennel and celery and another 2 tablespoons of olive oil, and cook for 8 to 10 minutes more, until the vegetables are soft but not coloured. Add the potato and 2 more tablespoons of oil and cook for another 2 minutes, then add the passata.

Add the brandy and Pernod, cook for a further 2 minutes, then add the bisque, star anise and ajillo and simmer until reduced by half.

While the bisque is reducing, heat 4 tablespoons of olive oil in a large sauté pan or heavy-bottomed frying pan over a medium heat until almost smoking. Add the lobster claws and cook for 2 minutes, then add the lobster bodies, flesh side down, and cook for 3 to 4 minutes more. Turn the bodies and claws over and cook for a further 2 minutes. Season with salt and pepper, then remove all the lobster pieces from the pan and set aside to keep warm.

Heat another 4 tablespoons of olive oil in the pan you cooked the lobster in, and add the monkfish. Let it colour for 1 minute on each side, then add the squid and prawns, season with salt and pepper and cook for a further 3 minutes. Remove the pan from the heat and set aside.

12 large raw king prawns, shell on
4 slices of sourdough bread, 1cm thick
a small bunch of tarragon
a bunch of fresh flat-leaf
parsley, finely chopped

Heat 4 tablespoons of olive oil in a large frying pan over a medium heat. Add the sourdough slices and toast on each side until golden brown. Remove from the pan and rub both sides of the bread with the remaining whole garlic clove, cut in half.

When the bisque has reduced by half, season if necessary with salt and pepper and add the tarragon and parsley. Add all the seafood to the soup and heat through over a medium heat for 2 to 3 minutes.

Serve the soup in bowls with the sourdough toast, making sure everyone gets their share of the seafood.

MEAT

At Barrafina we use all sorts of different cuts of meat. Whether we're using the expensive, lean cuts such as fillet and loin, or cheaper cuts like pig's trotters and lamb's brains, the provenance of the meat is vital. We firmly believe that if you are going to be a carnivore it is important that the animals you eat have had the best possible life. This is true not only for moral reasons but also because without exception animals with plenty of space, slow growth, good feed and a bit of love taste better.

Supermarkets have improved their meat offering a little in recent years, but apart from free-range organic chicken we would always buy our meat from a good-quality butcher. You'll need a good butcher when it comes to cooking with the more exotic cuts of meat from this chapter.

A couple of recipes here call for specific Spanish fresh cuts of meat such as Iberian pork or milk-fed lamb. These are available in the UK if you know where to look. The best place to start if you don't have a good Spanish butcher near you is on the internet; many suppliers now deliver straight to your door. See page 244 for a list of suppliers.

CHICKEN WINGS WITH GARLIC AND LEMON

We are never happier than when gnawing on a bowlful of hot, garlicky, lemony chicken wings. We feel that, like the sausage, these are best eaten far too hot, so that their consumption has to be accompanied by sharp sucking noises to prevent the mouth from burning. All non-greedy weirdos can ignore this peculiar advice. Here are two versions, version 1 for those wary of deep-frying.

SERVES 4 AS A TAPA

FOR VERSION 1
125ml olive oil
1kg chicken wings (about 12–16)
Maldon salt and freshly
ground black pepper
2 tablespoons dried red chilli flakes
4 garlic cloves, finely chopped
a large handful of fresh flat-leaf
parsley, chopped
juice of 1 lemon

FOR VERSION 2
the last 6 ingredients above, plus:
1 litre oil for deep-frying
100g special flour for deep-frying
(see page 17)

VERSION 1
Heat the oil in a large, heavy-bottomed frying pan until hot. Add the chicken wings, season well with salt and pepper and cook until golden brown and crisp. When the wings are almost ready, add the chilli flakes, garlic and parsley and cook for 1 more minute. Add the lemon juice, remove from the heat and stir well.

For the brave, this dish benefits from being eaten while still finger-burningly hot.

VERSION 2
Heat the oil for deep-frying to 180°C in a large pan or a deep-fryer. Dust the wings with the special flour and deep-fry for 10 minutes, until cooked through and golden brown. Remove, drain on kitchen paper and season with salt and pepper.

In a mixing bowl combine the chilli flakes, garlic, parsley and lemon juice. Add the chicken and stir well. Serve immediately.

CHICKEN WITH ROMESCO SAUCE

Barrafina's most regular customer, Mike 'Mustachio' Goldman, has eaten with us over 500 times in the last three years. He often requests that we feature this dish as one of our specials, as it is a particular favourite of his. Needless to say, we often oblige. Romesco Sauce is one of our favourite Spanish sauces, a heady mix of chillies, peppers, garlic and nuts, sweetened and sharpened with tomatoes and vinegar.

SERVES 4 AS A MAIN

4 x 150g chicken drumsticks
4 x 160g chicken thighs
1 tablespoon olive oil
Maldon salt and freshly ground black pepper
½ recipe quantity of Romesco Sauce (see page 214)
20g toasted flaked almonds

Preheat the oven to 200°C/400°F/gas 6. Put the chicken into a roasting tray. Drizzle it with olive oil, season it with salt and pepper and cook in the oven for 30 to 40 minutes, until cooked through and golden brown.

Gently warm the romesco sauce in a small pan and serve with the chicken, with the nuts sprinkled over the top.

GRILLED QUAIL WITH ALIOLI

We are great fans of quail, and when thinking about what to cook for friends it makes a satisfying change from chicken. Sadly the French have the edge over the Spanish when it comes to quail, and the best come from France.

SERVES 4 AS A TAPA OR 2 AS A MAIN

4 quail, spatchcocked
2 whole star anise
4 cloves
4 bay leaves, fresh if possible
6–7 sprigs of fresh thyme
1 teaspoon whole white peppercorns
100ml olive oil
Maldon salt and freshly ground black pepper
1 recipe quantity of Alioli (see page 207)

Place the quail, star anise, cloves, bay leaves, thyme, peppercorns and olive oil in a shallow dish. Mix well and leave to marinate in the fridge for a couple of hours, preferably overnight.

Heat a griddle pan until very hot. Remove the quail from the marinade and grill skin side down for 3 to 4 minutes, seasoning well with salt and pepper. Turn them over and grill for another 1½ to 2 minutes, then remove from the pan and serve with a large dollop of alioli.

QUAIL IN ESCABECHE

When Nieves suddenly remembered this old favourite from back home in the Basque Country, her eyes lit up and a large smile radiated across her face. As we ate the quail later that day it was easy to see why. The inclusion of all the delicious herbs is particularly good.

SERVES 4 AS A TAPA OR 2 AS A MAIN

FOR THE QUAIL
4 quail, spatchcocked
Maldon salt and freshly
ground black pepper

FOR THE ESCABECHE
400ml olive oil
200ml Moscatel vinegar
a large handful of each, or a selection,
of the following fresh herbs: sage,
tarragon, mint, thyme, parsley,
rosemary and coriander
6 bay leaves, fresh if possible
20g pinenuts
100g sultanas
100g dried apricots
100g stoned dried prunes

Put all the ingredients for the escabeche into a large pan. Warm very gently for 10 minutes, then set aside. If you let the heat rise too much, all the delicate aromatics will be destroyed. Pour the warm escabeche into a bowl.

Heat a griddle pan until very hot. Grill the quail for about 3 to 4 minutes, skin side down, then turn and cook the other side for 1½ to 2 minutes, or until done. Put the hot quail straight into the escabeche and leave to infuse for 20 to 30 minutes in a warmish place, turning them halfway through.

Remove the quail from the escabeche and place on serving plates, spooning some of the fruits and herbs on top of each bird. Season well with salt and pepper and serve.

FILLET OF BEEF WITH CARAMELIZED ONIONS

We would usually eat a fattier, more flavoursome cut of beef, but that said, there are moments when only the tenderness of a melt-in-your-mouth piece of fillet will do. Try to source a really well-hung (at least 28 days) piece of beef from your butcher.

SERVES 4 AS A MAIN

300ml ruby port
500ml Veal Stock (see page 213)
10 tablespoons olive oil
25g unsalted butter
250g baby onions, peeled
Maldon salt and freshly
ground black pepper
a small bunch of fresh thyme
400g new potatoes, cooked until
soft and cut in half lengthways
2 shallots, peeled and finely chopped
4 tablespoons finely chopped fresh chives
4 x 150g best beef fillet steaks,
cut into medallions

Put the port into a small pan and bring to the boil, then simmer over a medium heat until it has reduced by three-quarters. Add the veal stock and reduce until the liquid is thick enough to just coat the back of a spoon. Set aside.

Put 2 tablespoons of olive oil and the butter into a sauté pan or heavy-bottomed frying pan over a medium heat. Add the baby onions, season with salt and pepper and cook gently for 5 minutes. Add the thyme and cook for a further 15 to 20 minutes, until the onions are golden brown all over, then remove them from the pan and set aside.

Add 4 tablespoons of olive oil to the pan and put it over a medium heat. Add the potatoes, skin side up, and cook for 2 minutes. Add the shallots, mix well, season with salt and pepper and add the chopped chives. Set aside and keep warm.

Heat 4 tablespoons of olive oil in a separate sauté pan or heavy-bottomed frying pan over a medium heat until smoking. Add the beef fillets and cook for 30 seconds on each side, turning to seal the surface of the meat. Now cook further, depending on whether you like your beef well done, medium or rare (about 1 minute more each side for rare, 2 for medium rare, 3 for well done).

Add the baby onions to the port sauce and heat through. Put the beef on serving plates and spoon over the sauce, with the potatoes alongside.

BEEF STEW

We serve this in Barrafina as a one-pot wonder in small black cast-iron dishes. During the winter months the fine smell, and the sight of the steam coming off as these pots emerge from the oven, are enough to get the whole bar clamouring for one of their own.

SERVES 4–6 AS A MAIN

60ml extra virgin olive oil
1kg best-quality braising beef, cut into 4cm cubes
Maldon salt and freshly ground black pepper
4 garlic cloves, peeled and finely sliced
2 carrots, peeled and cut into 1cm dice
½ a celeriac, peeled and cut into 1cm dice
2 parsnips, peeled and cut into 1cm dice
3 large shallots, peeled and chopped
2 leeks (white and light green part only), cut into 1cm dice
a small bunch of fresh thyme
4 bay leaves, fresh if possible
1½ bottles of red wine
3 litres Chicken Stock (see page 208)
1 Savoy cabbage, core removed, heart finely sliced

Heat 30ml of olive oil in a large casserole over a medium heat. When the oil is smoking, add the beef, season with salt and pepper and cook on all sides for about 15 minutes, until nicely browned. Remove from the casserole and set aside.

Put another 30ml of olive oil into the casserole, add the garlic and cook gently for 2 to 3 minutes without colouring. Add the carrots, cook for 1 minute, then add the celeriac and parsnips and cook for 2 minutes more. Add the shallots and leeks, stirring continuously, then add the thyme and bay leaves and cook for a further 15 minutes.

Pour in the red wine and cook over a high heat until it has reduced by half. Add the chicken stock, then the beef. Reduce the heat a little and simmer for 20 minutes, uncovered, removing any scum that rises to the top. Cover the casserole with a lid or foil and cook for 2 hours, then uncover and simmer for a further 15 to 20 minutes, until the sauce starts to thicken.

Bring a large pan of salted water to the boil. Add the cabbage and cook for 2 to 3 minutes, then drain and season with salt and pepper. Stir in a splash of olive oil.

Serve the stew in bowls, with the cabbage on top.

SLOW-COOKED OXTAIL

We love making these slow-cooked dishes on a Sunday morning at home. You can put them into the oven after breakfast, then head off into the wide open spaces until lunchtime without having to worry about over-cooking the lunch. Provided the temperature is set nice and low, the oxtail can easily stay in the oven for another hour if you come home late.

SERVES 4 AS A MAIN

150ml olive oil
1.5kg oxtail
75g plain flour for dusting
4 garlic cloves, peeled and finely sliced
3 large shallots,
peeled and finely chopped
2 carrots, peeled and cut into 1cm dice
2 leeks (white part only), finely chopped
2 sticks of celery, cut into 1cm dice
4 bay leaves, fresh if possible
a small bunch of fresh thyme
Maldon salt and freshly
ground black pepper
1 bottle of red wine
2 litres Chicken Stock
(see page 208)

Heat 3 tablespoons of the oil in a large pan or casserole over a medium heat until almost smoking. Dust the pieces of oxtail in the flour, ensuring they have a fine coating all over. Shake off the excess, then add the oxtail to the pan and cook for 5 minutes. Turn it over and cook for a further 5 minutes, then remove from the oil, drain on kitchen paper and set aside.

Add another 3 tablespoons of oil to the pan. Add the garlic and shallots and cook gently for 2 minutes. Add the carrots, cook for 2 minutes, then add the leeks and celery and cook for a further minute. Add the bay leaves and thyme and season with salt and pepper.

Pour in the red wine and chicken stock and add the oxtail. Bring to the boil, then lower the heat to a simmer. Make a cartouche (a circular sheet of baking parchment with a 3cm hole in the centre that fits the pan and covers the ingredients) and lay it over the meat, then cover the pan with foil and cook for 3 hours over a low heat.

When the time is up, remove the foil and cartouche. Take the pieces of oxtail out of the pan and keep them warm. Skim off the fat from the liquid in the pan, then boil until it has reduced and thickened. Return the oxtail pieces to the pan and simmer for 5 to 10 minutes to thicken the sauce – you should have about 250–350ml left at the end.

Serve the oxtail in bowls, with the sauce poured over.

OXTAIL WITH SCALLOPS

This is a perfect dish to make if you have a little oxtail left over from another day. Provided you have some oxtail already cooked, it will take only a few minutes to prepare and will satisfy even your most demanding dinner companions. For anyone who has the energy to cook oxtail especially for this dish – we raise our hats to your dedication.

SERVES 4 AS A TAPA

½ recipe quantity of Slow-cooked Oxtail (see page 125)
150ml Pedro Ximénez balsamic vinegar
1 dried choricero pepper (see page 18), soaked in warm water for 2 hours
a drizzle of olive oil
8 diver-caught scallops, cleaned and prepared
Maldon salt and freshly ground black pepper

Remove the oxtail pieces from the sauce and put the sauce and vegetables into a pan with a little water. Strip all the meat off the oxtail and shred coarsely. Add it to the pan of sauce and reheat gently.

Put the Pedro Ximénez balsamic vinegar into a small pan and bring to the boil. Simmer until reduced by two-thirds.

Drain the choricero pepper, then remove the seeds and finely slice.

Heat a frying pan until very hot. Add a good slosh of oil, then the scallops, and cook them for 2 minutes on each side, seasoning them with salt and pepper as you go.

On each serving plate drizzle a little of the Pedro Ximénez reduction, then a good spoonful of oxtail, and on top of that place the scallops. Finish with a couple of slices of choricero.

ARROCINA BEANS WITH CHORIZO, MORCILLA AND PORK BELLY

This is one of our very favourite winter dishes. It works brilliantly as a one-pot wonder and can be enjoyed over several days, as it carries on getting better and better. Many a broken man has been mended at Barrafina after devouring this dish – it has that sort of effect. Arrocina beans are tiny white beans grown in the Gredos mountains of Spain. Remember to soak them overnight.

SERVES 6–8 AS A MAIN

500g top-quality pork belly
4–5 dessertspoons extra virgin olive oil
Maldon salt and freshly ground black pepper
1 teaspoon cumin seeds
2 fennel bulbs, cut into 1cm dice
2 medium carrots, peeled and cut into 1cm dice
2 large shallots, peeled and diced
1 large leek, cut into 1cm dice
2 sticks of celery, cut into 1cm dice
1 head of garlic, cloves peeled and finely chopped
150g morcilla curada (see page 43)
3 dried choricero peppers (see page 18), soaked in warm water for 2 hours
3 dried guindilla chillies, cut in half lengthways
5 bay leaves, fresh if possible
a small bunch of fresh thyme
500g Arrocina beans, soaked in cold water overnight
2 litres Chicken Stock (see page 208)
800g cooking chorizo, sliced
150g morcilla de Burgos (see page 43), skin removed, sliced
1 Savoy cabbage, core removed, heart finely sliced and lightly cooked

Preheat the oven to 180°C/350°F/gas 4. Rub the meaty side of the pork belly with a little of the olive oil and season it with salt, pepper and cumin seeds. Put it into a large roasting tray, skin side down, and roast in the oven for 2 hours. Remove from the oven and cut the pork belly into 3cm strips across its width. Set aside.

Meanwhile, heat a large pan or casserole over a medium heat and add 2 dessertspoons of olive oil. Add the vegetables and garlic and cook gently, stirring, for 10 minutes.

Peel the morcilla curada and crumble it into the casserole with your hands. Drain the choricero peppers and slice, removing the seeds. Add the choriceros, chillies, bay leaves and thyme to the casserole and cook for a further 2 minutes. Add the drained Arrocina beans and the chicken stock and simmer very gently, uncovered, for 1½ hours, stirring occasionally, until the beans are cooked and beautifully soft.

Heat a dessertspoon of olive oil in a frying pan over a medium heat. Add the chorizo and morcilla de Burgos and cook for 5 to 6 minutes, then add to the stew.

Finally add the sliced pork belly and cooked Savoy cabbage, season with salt and pepper, and serve.

IBERIAN PIG'S CHEEKS WITH CELERIAC PURÉE AND PARSNIP CRISPS

This is a wonderfully comforting winter dish. Iberian pig's cheeks are particularly good, and you can get them in the UK occasionally (see page 244), but cheeks from other happy pigs work well too.

SERVES 4 AS A MAIN

8 dessertspoons good-quality olive oil
1kg pig's cheeks
Maldon salt and freshly ground black pepper
4 garlic cloves, peeled and sliced
3 large shallots, peeled and finely chopped
2 carrots, peeled and cut into 1 cm dice
2 leeks (just the white part), finely chopped
2 sticks of celery, finely chopped
4 bay leaves, fresh if possible
a small bunch of fresh thyme
1 bottle of red wine
600ml Chicken Stock (see page 208)
1 recipe quantity of Celeriac Purée (see page 198)

FOR THE PARSNIP CRISPS
1 litre oil for deep-frying
2 parsnips

Heat 5 dessertspoons of olive oil over a medium heat in a large casserole or pan until almost smoking. Add the pig's cheeks and season with salt and pepper. Cook for 6 to 7 minutes, then turn the cheeks over, season again, and cook for a further 2 minutes. Remove the cheeks and set aside.

Add the garlic and shallots and cook for 2 minutes, then add 3 more dessertspoons of olive oil. Add the carrots and cook for 1 minute, then add the leeks and celery and cook for a further minute. Add the bay leaves and thyme.

Add the wine and simmer over a medium heat until it has almost all disappeared. Add the stock and the pig's cheeks and bring back to the boil. Place a cartouche (a circular sheet of baking parchment with a 3cm hole in the centre that covers the ingredients) over the pig's cheeks and simmer on a low heat for 2 hours.

To make the parsnip crisps, heat the oil for deep-frying to 180°C in a large pan or a deep-fryer. Peel the parsnips and then, using a vegetable peeler, shave long strips along their length, stopping when you get to the core. Carefully lower the strips into the hot oil and fry for 2 minutes, stirring regularly to prevent them sticking. Remove and drain on kitchen paper, then season with salt.

When the pig's cheeks are ready, take the casserole off the heat and skim off and discard any fat that has risen to the surface. The sauce should be thick – if it isn't, remove the cheeks and keep warm while you simmer the liquid until it is reduced, thick and flavoursome.

Put the celeriac purée into a pan and reheat gently. Serve with the pig's cheeks and the parsnip crisps.

PIG'S TROTTER FRITTERS

There is something very satisfying about preparing pig's trotters from scratch. The recipe looks lengthy, and the trotters do need to be cooked for a long time, but the result is delicious. Take care that no little fragments of bone are left behind when you debone the trotters.

SERVES 8 AS A TAPA

6 pig's trotters
2 carrots, peeled and cut into 3cm dice
2 leeks, roughly chopped
3 celery sticks, cut into 3cm dice
2 large white onions, peeled and roughly chopped
4 bay leaves, fresh if possible
a small bunch of fresh thyme
7 garlic cloves, peeled
7 tablespoons extra virgin olive oil
500g fresh chanterelle mushrooms
2 large shallots, peeled and finely chopped
1 tablespoon fresh thyme leaves
500g large raw prawns, peeled and cut into 1cm dice
salt and freshly ground black pepper
2 tablespoons finely chopped fresh flat-leaf parsley
2 free-range eggs
100g plain flour
1 litre oil for deep-frying

Put the trotters, carrots, leeks, celery, onions, bay leaves, bunch of thyme and 5 of the garlic cloves into a large pan and fill with cold water. Bring to the boil over a medium heat, removing and discarding any scum that appears. Reduce the heat and simmer for 3 hours (topping up with boiling water from the kettle if necessary). Remove from the heat and set aside to cool.

Preheat the oven to 180°C/350°F/gas 4. Transfer the trotters and 500ml of their liquid to a large oven tray. Cover with foil and cook for 1 hour in the oven (in two batches if you can't fit everything into one tray). Remove from the oven and allow to cool.

Heat 3 tablespoons of olive oil in a large sauté pan or heavy-bottomed frying pan over a medium heat. Add the mushrooms and cook gently for 10 to 12 minutes, stirring occasionally. Add the shallots and another tablespoon of olive oil and mix well. Add the remaining garlic cloves, chopped, and 1 tablespoon of fresh thyme leaves, and cook for a further 2 minutes. Add the prawns and 3 tablespoons of olive oil and mix well. Season with salt and pepper and cook for a further couple of minutes, until the prawns have turned pink. Add the parsley and stir well, then remove from the heat and allow to cool.

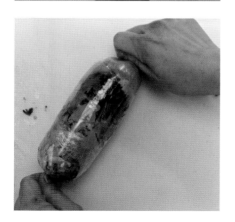

Remove the trotters from their juices and put them on a board. Very carefully run your thumb down the underside of each trotter, opening up the skin and removing all the cartilage and bone. Try to keep the skin and meat as much as possible intact in large pieces. Make sure there are no bones left in the trotter meat by running your fingers over the meat and gently pressing down.

On a large piece of clingfilm, about 40 x 40cm, start to lay out the trotter meat to form a flat seamless 10 x 10cm square (you should get 4 or 5 of these squares from the meat). Season lightly with salt and pepper. Spoon the prawn and mushroom mixture into the middle of each pig's trotter square.

Taking the end of the clingfilm closest to you, fold the trotter over the top of the prawns and mushrooms and roll into a relatively tight sausage. Be careful not to get the clingfilm inside the sausage. Taking the ends firmly between thumb and forefinger, roll the sausage tightly so that it takes on a good firm cylindrical shape. Tie knots in the ends and refrigerate overnight.

With an extremely sharp knife, slice off a sliver from each end of the trotter sausage and discard. Leaving the clingfilm on, slice the sausage extremely carefully into 3cm rounds, being careful not to lose any filling. Now remove the clingfilm very carefully.

Beat the eggs and pour on to a flat plate. Gently flour the trotter slices and roll in the beaten egg. Heat the oil to 180°C in a large pan or a deep-fryer. Deep-fry the fritters for 1 minute, then gently turn them over and cook until golden brown. You may need to do them in batches. Remove and drain on kitchen paper.

Season with salt and pepper and serve with a spicy tomato sauce (see page 160).

PORK CUTLETS WITH CAULIFLOWER PURÉE

This is a wonderful combination of flavours – the smoked paprika, cauliflower and pork – but what will make or break the dish is sourcing really good cutlets from a happy pig. We use a brilliant farmer, Richard Vaughan, who raises and sells fantastic meat (see page 245). Sourcing rare breeds and using a butcher you know and trust makes all the difference.

SERVES 4 AS A MAIN

FOR THE PORK
8 small or 4 large pork cutlets
Maldon salt and freshly ground black pepper
2 dessertspoons ground cumin
2 dessertspoons sweet smoked paprika
2 dessertspoons dried oregano
½ teaspoon cayenne pepper
10 garlic cloves, peeled and flattened with the back of a knife
4 bay leaves, fresh if possible
a bunch of fresh thyme
200ml olive oil

FOR THE CAULIFLOWER PURÉE
2 cauliflowers
2 litres water
500ml milk
3 bay leaves, fresh if possible
25ml olive oil
40g unsalted butter
20g toasted flaked almonds

Put all the ingredients for the pork into a large bowl and mix well. Cover with clingfilm and leave to marinate in the fridge for a minimum of 4 hours, or overnight.

Trim the base from the cauliflowers and roughly separate the florets. Put them into a large pan with the water and milk, add the bay leaves, bring to the boil and cook for 30 minutes, until very tender. Drain off the liquid and remove 2 of the bay leaves. Blitz the cauliflower in a food processor with the remaining bay leaf, plenty of salt and pepper, the olive oil and the butter until smooth. Transfer the cauliflower purée to an ovenproof dish, cover with foil and keep warm in a low oven while you cook the cutlets.

Heat a heavy-bottomed frying pan or griddle pan until very hot. Remove the pork from the marinade and pan-fry or griddle it for about 5 minutes on each side, seasoning with a little salt and pepper on both sides as you go. Holding the pork with tongs, turn it so that the thin, fatty edge is face down and hold it there to crisp up the outside for another 5 minutes or so. This will involve a bit of a balancing act but the results make it well worthwhile.

When the cutlets are ready, remove them from the heat to a warmed plate and let them rest for 5 minutes or so. Sprinkle the cauliflower purée with the toasted nuts and serve with the cutlets.

ROAST LEG OF MIDDLE WHITE PORK

The Middle White had all but disappeared in Britain before dedicated farmers such as our friend Richard Vaughan brought it back from the brink. The rationing of the Second World War was to blame for Danish imports and bacon pigs being preferred. The Middle White is an excellent 'pork pig', and so admired by the Japanese that in the 1930s Emperor Hirohito would eat only Middle White and even erected a statue to the splendid beast. This dish brings out the best of what is a very fine meat.

SERVES 10–12 AS A MAIN

5 dessertspoons good-quality olive oil
1 x 4kg leg of Middle White pork
8 garlic cloves, peeled and crushed
a bunch of fresh thyme
Maldon salt and freshly ground black pepper
1 dessertspoon ground cumin

FOR THE SAUCE
200g best-quality membrillo or quince paste
50ml water
500ml Veal Stock (see page 213)

FOR THE BABY SPINACH SALAD
400g baby spinach leaves
2 large shallots, peeled and finely chopped
50ml extra virgin olive oil
50ml Moscatel vinegar

Preheat the oven to 180°C/350°F/gas 4. Pour 4 dessert-spoons of olive oil into a large roasting tray and tip the tray so that the oil greases it all over. Score the skin of the pork leg in lines 1cm apart and put it into the tray. Stuff the garlic and thyme into the score lines, then drizzle the leg with another dessertspoon of olive oil and season with salt and pepper. Sprinkle with the cumin.

Put the pork into the oven and roast for 45 minutes. Then turn the oven down to 140°C/275°F/gas 1 and roast for a further 2¾ hours. Take out of the oven and leave to rest for 20 minutes or so.

When you are nearly ready to serve the pork, make the sauce. Put the membrillo or quince paste into a small pan with the water and place over a medium heat until it has melted. Add the veal stock and simmer until the sauce starts to thicken and take on a gloss.

Put the spinach, shallots, olive oil and vinegar into a large serving bowl and mix well. Season to taste with salt and pepper.

Carve the pork and drizzle with the sauce. Serve with the spinach salad.

SUCKLING PIG

For this, you will need the largest roasting tray you can fit into your oven. If the suckling pig does not fit into the oven whole, there is nothing wrong with cutting the animal in half and then piecing it back together for the grand presentation. We use Segovian suckling pigs at Barrafina, but these days it is possible to source small English piglets (see our list of suppliers on page 244). Your butcher should be able to order you a suckling pig if you give him a few days' notice.

SERVES 10–12 AS A MAIN

a small bunch of fresh thyme
7 garlic cloves, peeled and halved
7 bay leaves, fresh if possible
juice of 2 lemons
1 x 5–6kg suckling pig
Maldon salt and freshly
ground black pepper
4 dessertspoons good-quality olive oil
1.5 litres Chicken Stock (see page 208)
10 sprigs of fresh mint, leaves chopped

Preheat the oven to 180°C/350°F/gas 4. Scatter the thyme, garlic, bay leaves and lemon juice over your large roasting tray.

Dry the cavity of the pig with kitchen paper to make sure there is no blood remaining. Season the cavity generously with salt and pepper. Place the pig in the tray, cavity down (right way up) and cover the head, snout and ears with foil. Massage the oil into the skin of the pig and season with pepper.

Warm the stock in a pan. Pour it into the oven tray, around and not over the pig. Roast the pig in the oven for 25 minutes, then turn the temperature down to 140°C/275°F/gas 1 and roast for a further 2½ hours.

Remove the pig from the oven. Take it out of the tray, put it on to a platter or board, cover with foil and leave to rest.

Drain all the cooking juices and stock from the tray into a pan, add the mint and bring to a simmer. Cook until the juices have reduced by two-thirds, skimming off any fat from the surface, then strain the sauce into a jug.

Carve the suckling pig and serve with the sauce.

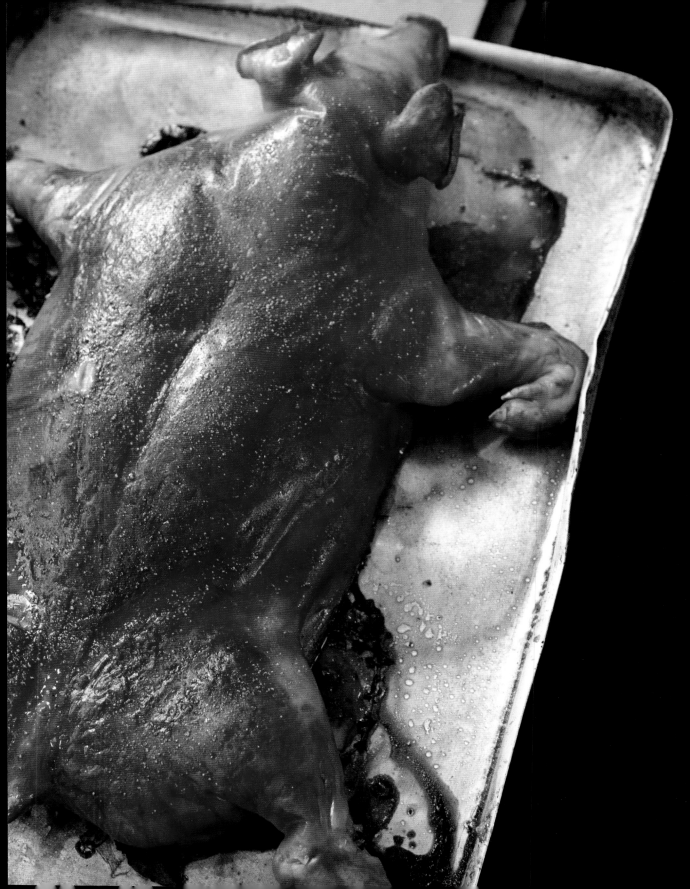

COCHEFRITO

This is a very fine way to use up leftover suckling pig, or indeed any leftover roast pork. We suggest you eat it in the company of somebody who likes chewing bones and is happy to eat with their fingers.

SERVES 4 AS A TAPA OR 2 AS A MAIN

2 tablespoons olive oil
300g leftover suckling pig, chopped into 5–6cm cubes (use a large hatchet or heavy knife)
Maldon salt and freshly ground black pepper
2 bay leaves, fresh if possible
1 whole head of garlic, halved horizontally
a handful of fresh thyme sprigs
1 teaspoon paprika
1 teaspoon ground cumin
1 teaspoon dried oregano

Heat the oil in a large, heavy-bottomed frying pan until smoking. Add the piggy pieces, season with salt and pepper and fry for 2 minutes. Add the bay leaves, garlic and thyme and continue to fry until the pig is nice and crispy. Keep stirring all the time to stop it sticking.

When the pig is done, add the paprika, cumin and oregano and cook for another minute. Remove from the heat and serve with plenty of napkins.

TXISTORRA WITH DUCK EGG AND BABY POTATOES

This is a like a Spanish version of the full English breakfast and is guaranteed to give strength even to those severely out of sorts. It could be eaten at any time of the day, but is fairly substantial so you won't need much else afterwards. Txistorra is a thin chorizo that comes wound into a spiral and is available from good Spanish delis. A good-quality cooking chorizo would make a fine substitute. Wild garlic is common in the UK in the spring and can be found on grass verges and in woodland. If you do not have time to forage, it can be bought from specialists online (see page 244).

SERVES 4 AS A LARGE BREAKFAST,
BRUNCH OR SUNDAY DINNER

Maldon salt and freshly ground black pepper
400g baby new potatoes
180ml extra virgin olive oil, plus extra for drizzling
2 large shallots, peeled and finely chopped
200g wild garlic leaves or spinach
150–160g txistorra or good-quality cooking chorizo, cut into 4cm pieces
240g morcilla de Burgos (see page 43), skin removed, cut into 2cm pieces
4 duck eggs
½ teaspoon sweet smoked paprika

Bring a large pan of salted water to the boil. Add the potatoes and cook for about 10 to 12 minutes, or until soft, then drain and cut in half lengthways.

Heat 60ml of olive oil in a large sauté pan or heavy-bottomed frying pan over a medium heat until almost smoking. Add the potatoes and sauté until golden brown all over. Add the shallots and mix well, then add the wild garlic leaves or spinach and cook gently until they are soft. Remove from the heat and keep warm.

In a separate frying pan heat 80ml of olive oil over a medium heat until almost smoking. Add the txistorra and cook for 2 minutes, turning occasionally, then add the morcilla and cook for 2 minutes on each side. Remove from the heat.

Meanwhile, heat the remaining 40ml of olive oil in a small frying pan and fry the duck eggs.

Serve the potatoes and txistorra with the duck eggs on top, dusted with a little sweet smoked paprika, salt and pepper and drizzled with extra virgin olive oil.

CHORIZO, POTATO AND WATERCRESS SALAD

Chorizo is one of those things that while very delicious by itself is best appreciated when combined with something else. We came up with this dish when we first opened Barrafina, and it has been on the menu ever since. Indeed, a small riot might ensue on Frith Street should we ever decide to give it a rest.

SERVES 4 AS A LIGHT LUNCH

Maldon salt and freshly ground black pepper
400g new potatoes, cooked and halved lengthways
5 tablespoons olive oil
240g small cooking chorizos
40g butter
4 tablespoons chopped shallots
4 tablespoons chopped fresh flat-leaf parsley
60g watercress

Bring a large pan of salted water to the boil. Add the potatoes and cook for about 10 to 12 minutes, or until soft, then drain and cut in half lengthways.

Heat an overhead grill to medium high. In a heavy-bottomed frying pan, heat 4 tablespoons of olive oil until beginning to smoke. Add the potatoes, season with salt and pepper and cook until nicely golden brown.

While the potatoes are browning, split the chorizos in half lengthways and score the cut side with a crosshatch about 1mm deep. Grill for 2 to 3 minutes on each side.

Add the butter and shallots to the potatoes and cook for another 5 minutes. Stir in the parsley and remove from the heat.

Drizzle the watercress with the remaining tablespoon of olive oil, sprinkle with a pinch of salt and serve with the potatoes and the grilled chorizo. You can spoon a little of the oil from the chorizo on to the potatoes for extra oomph if you like.

MORCILLA, PIQUILLO PEPPERS AND QUAIL'S EGGS

This dish is as pretty as a picture and extremely delicious too. To crack the quail's eggs, use a small sharp knife to make a little hole in the shell before breaking in the traditional fashion. Morcilla is Spanish black pudding and is available from good Spanish delis. There are many different kinds, all of which will work with this dish, but at Barrafina we use morcilla choricera, which is a half-chorizo half-morcilla mix. It goes without saying that it's Ibérico.

SERVES 4 AS A TAPA

7 tablespoons extra virgin olive oil, plus extra for drizzling
1 x 390g tin or jar of piquillo peppers (see page 18), drained and roughly chopped
200g morcilla choricera (see page 43), cut into 1.5cm rounds
8 quail's eggs
Maldon salt and freshly ground black pepper
½ tablespoon chopped fresh flat-leaf parsley

Heat the grill to a medium high heat. Put 4 tablespoons of olive oil into a small pan over a low heat, add the piquillo peppers, and warm them through, being careful not to let them colour.

Put the morcilla slices on a metal tray and place under the hot grill, about 10cm from the heat, until they start to release their natural oils and become squidgy around the edges.

Heat 3 more tablespoons of olive oil in a small non-stick frying pan and fry the quail's eggs for about 2 minutes. Season with salt and pepper.

To serve, place 2 spoonfuls of the piquillo peppers on each serving plate. Put the grilled morcilla on top, and finally arrange the fried quail's eggs on top of the morcilla. Drizzle with a little extra virgin olive oil and sprinkle with the chopped parsley.

BRAISED LEG OF MILK-FED LAMB WITH MANZANILLA

Not only is sherry a fabulous drink, it is also brilliant to cook with. Unlike white wine, it adds neither sweetness nor fruitiness but just a wonderful savoury touch. After years of deliberation we have decided that we much prefer milk-fed lamb cooked slowly and cooked right through, not pink as we would insist for grown-up lamb. Milk-fed lamb is gelatinous and requires different treatment. Ask your butcher to order you milk-fed lamb, as it is becoming easier to get hold of (see page 244). If he can't help you, this recipe will work with a normal leg of lamb – it will just require a longer cooking time.

SERVES 4 AS A MAIN

4–5 tablespoons olive oil
2 whole legs of milk-fed lamb, about 500g each
Maldon salt and freshly ground black pepper
3 shallots, peeled and quartered lengthways
8 garlic cloves, peeled and flattened with the back of a knife
a large handful of fresh thyme
6 bay leaves, fresh if possible
200ml manzanilla sherry
a good-sized bunch of watercress
a little extra virgin olive oil

Preheat the oven to 180°C/350°F/gas 4. Put 4 tablespoons of olive oil into a heavy-bottomed casserole and heat until smoking. Add the lamb and sear on all sides until deep brown, seasoning with salt and pepper as you go.

Remove the lamb from the casserole, then turn down the heat a little and add the shallots, garlic, thyme and bay leaves. Add a little more olive oil if necessary and cook until the shallots and garlic are nicely coloured.

Add the sherry and deglaze the casserole over a high heat, scraping all the caramelized bits from the bottom. Return the lamb to the casserole. Put the lid on and cook in the oven for 45 minutes, then turn the oven temperature down to 140°C/275°F/gas 1 and cook for another 2½ hours. The lamb should be beginning to fall off the bone at this stage.

Take the lamb out of the casserole and keep it warm. Put the casserole on a medium heat and simmer until the liquid has reduced by three-quarters. Taste the sauce and adjust the seasoning if necessary.

Carve the lamb on to serving plates and drizzle with the sauce. Toss the watercress with a little olive oil and serve with the lamb.

LAMB CUTLETS WITH AJO BLANCO AND BLACK OLIVES

Ajo blanco is usually served as a cold soup in Spain, as an alternative to gazpacho, but this slightly thickened version makes an excellent accompaniment to lamb. If the weather is fine, cooking the cutlets on the barbecue lends a great smokiness to the meat that further improves the combination.

SERVES 4 AS A MAIN

8–12 lamb cutlets, trimmed
1 tablespoon Ajillo (see page 206)

FOR THE AJO BLANCO
½ a large loaf of good-quality white bread, crusts removed
80g whole blanched almonds
1 garlic clove, peeled and flattened with the back of a knife
300ml milk
3 Granny Smith apples, peeled, cored and quartered
25ml Moscatel vinegar
150ml olive oil
Maldon salt and freshly ground black pepper

FOR THE OLIVES
20 pitted black Aragón olives
2 teaspoons capers, coarsely chopped
1–2 tablespoons olive oil

To make the ajo blanco, put the bread, almonds, garlic and milk into a large bowl, stir, then cover the bowl and leave in the fridge for a minimum of 1 hour, preferably overnight. Put the bread and milk mixture into a blender or food processor with the apples, Moscatel vinegar and olive oil and blend well. Season with salt and pepper and return the mixture to the fridge.

Roughly chop the olives and put into a bowl. Add the capers and the olive oil and set aside.

Heat a griddle pan until smoking and grill the lamb cutlets for about 3 minutes on each side, seasoning well with salt and pepper. Remove from the pan and leave to rest in a warm place for 10 minutes.

Place the cutlets on serving plates and drizzle a little ajillo on top. Place a generous dollop of ajo blanco to one side, and on top of the ajo blanco spoon a little of the chopped olive mixture.

RUMP OF LAMB WITH RED WINE SAUCE

Rump of lamb is an undervalued cut of meat that delivers both value and flavour. Don't forget to let the meat rest before serving. Papas a lo Pobre (see page 198) would make a fine accompaniment.

SERVES 4 AS A MAIN

4 x 125g pieces of best rump of lamb
4 tablespoons good-quality olive oil
Maldon salt

FOR THE SAUCE
250ml Veal Sauce (see page 213)
½ recipe quantity of Ajillo (see page 206)

Criss-cross the skin of the lamb with a sharp knife. Heat the olive oil in a sauté pan or heavy-bottomed frying pan over a medium heat, and sprinkle 2 good pinches of salt into the pan. Add the lamb, skin side down, and cook for 8 minutes, until golden brown. Turn the lamb over, then cook for a further 25 minutes, turning it every 5 minutes. Remove the lamb from the pan to a board and allow it to rest for at least 5 minutes.

Gently heat the veal sauce in a small pan. Carve the rump into 0.5cm slices and place on serving plates. Spoon over the sauce, drizzle over the ajillo and serve.

RABBIT STEW

We find it hard to imagine why most chefs prefer to use farmed rabbit when there are so many wild rabbits hopping around. Wild rabbits are delicious, though there is much less meat than on farmed rabbits – if you use wild rabbit you'll need two for this recipe.

SERVES 4–6 AS A MAIN

8 tablespoons olive oil
1 farmed rabbit, jointed into 8 pieces (ask the butcher)
Maldon salt and freshly ground black pepper
2 onions, peeled and sliced finely into half-moons
4 garlic cloves, finely sliced
3 dried choricero peppers, soaked in warm water for 2 hours (see page 18)
3 dried red chillies, soaked in warm water for 2 hours
4 teaspoons smoked paprika
1 tablespoon caster sugar
2 tablespoons tomato purée
8 medium tomatoes, diced
500g potatoes, cut into 2.5cm cubes
a small bunch of fresh thyme
3 bay leaves, fresh if possible
750ml Chicken Stock (see page 208)
8–12 tinned or jarred piquillo peppers (see page 18), drained and sliced
4 tablespoons chopped fresh chives
4 tablespoons chopped fresh flat-leaf parsley

Heat 4 tablespoons of olive oil in a large, heavy-bottomed casserole and fry the rabbit pieces until well browned. Season with salt and pepper, then remove the rabbit from the casserole and set aside. You will probably have to do this in two batches.

Add the rest of the olive oil to the pan and fry the onions and garlic for 10 minutes over a medium heat. Drain the dried red chillies and choriceros and remove the seeds, then slice them and add to the pan. Cook for another 5 minutes. Add the smoked paprika, sugar, tomato purée and diced tomatoes, with a little more oil if necessary, and continue to cook for another 15 minutes.

Add the potatoes, thyme, bay leaves, stock and the rabbit pieces. Bring to the boil, then reduce the heat to a gentle simmer and cook for 25 minutes, or until the potatoes are very tender. Add the piquillo peppers and cook for another 5 minutes.

Adjust the seasoning if necessary and serve the stew with the chives and parsley sprinkled over the top.

ARROZ CAMPERO

One of our absolute favourite dishes. It is basically a rabbit paella but enriched with wild mushrooms and delicious morcilla. We use morcilla de Burgos, but you can use other kinds of morcilla. In days gone by, farm labourers would knock this sort of thing up for lunch in a large paella pan over an open fire, washed down with a porrón or two of rustic red wine. Nothing wrong with that, we reckon! Payoyo is a cured ewe's milk cheese from Cádiz in the south of Spain and is similar to aged Manchego, which also works well.

SERVES 6 AS A MAIN

8 tablespoons good-quality olive oil
1 whole farmed rabbit, jointed into 12 pieces (ask the butcher)
Maldon salt and freshly ground black pepper
1kg fresh mixed mushrooms, roughly chopped: oyster, chestnut, blewits, chanterelles, girolles
8 bay leaves, fresh if possible
a small bunch of fresh thyme
2 large shallots, peeled and finely chopped
4 garlic cloves, peeled and finely sliced
2 leeks (only the white part), finely chopped
150g morcilla de Burgos (see page 43), skin removed
1.6 litres Chicken Stock (see page 208)
480g Calasparra or Bomba rice
50g Payoyo cheese or other ewe's milk cheese
2 tablespoons fresh flat-leaf parsley leaves, cut into thin strips

Heat 2 tablespoons of olive oil in a large sauté pan or heavy-bottomed frying pan over a medium heat, and when it is almost smoking, add the rabbit. Season with salt and pepper and cook for 3 to 4 minutes on each side, until nicely coloured. Remove the rabbit from the pan and set aside.

Add 4 more tablespoons of oil to the pan. Add the mushrooms and cook gently for 5 minutes, stirring occasionally. Add the bay leaves and thyme and cook for a further 4 to 5 minutes, then add 2 more tablespoons of oil and the shallots, garlic and leeks. Season with salt and pepper and cook for 4 to 5 minutes.

Remove the thyme and bay leaves from the pan, then crumble in the morcilla and pour in 125ml of the stock, stirring well. Add the rice and a little more of the stock, then put the rabbit back into the pan and mix well. Keep adding the stock bit by bit, stirring until it has all been absorbed.

When the rice is tender, season with salt and pepper. Shave the Payoyo or other ewe's milk cheese over the top, scatter with the parsley and serve.

LOIN OF VENISON WITH RED CABBAGE, PINENUTS AND SULTANAS

Traditionally red cabbage is cooked long and slow, until it begins to break down and becomes slightly mushy. This recipe takes a novel approach and just slightly warms the cabbage through, turning it into a crunchy, warm salad, at the same time sweet, sour and savoury – and very good it is too.

SERVES 4 AS A MAIN

60g pinenuts
60g sultanas
75ml Pedro Ximénez balsamic vinegar
16 dessertspoons olive oil
½ a red cabbage, core removed, heart very finely sliced
Maldon salt and freshly ground black pepper
600g loin or fillet of venison, trimmed of any sinews and cut into 4 slices
40g Payoyo or Manchego cheese

Preheat the oven to 180°C/350°F/gas 4. Put the pinenuts into a small roasting tray and toast them in the oven for about a minute, until lightly browned. Alternatively you can toast them in a small dry frying pan for a minute or so. Put the sultanas into a small bowl with the balsamic vinegar and set aside.

Heat 8 dessertspoons of olive oil in a large, deep, heavy-bottomed frying pan. Throw in the red cabbage, season with salt and pepper and cook for about 5 minutes, until heated through but still a little crunchy. Add the sultanas and most of their soaking vinegar, reserving a little, then stir in the pinenuts and cook for another minute or so.

While the cabbage is cooking, heat the rest of the oil in another heavy-bottomed frying pan until very hot. Add the venison slices and cook for about 1½ minutes on each side – they should still be rare – seasoning with salt and pepper as you go.

Place a large spoonful of red cabbage on each serving plate. Cut the venison steaks into strips and lay on top. Drizzle the venison with a little of the reserved soaking vinegar, and shave a couple of very thin slivers of Payoyo or Manchego over the top.

CRISP FRIED MILK-FED LAMB'S BRAINS WITH A SPICY TOMATO SAUCE

People can be frightened of cooking and eating brains, but in our view they should not be, as brains are delicious and easy to prepare. Lamb's brains are often sold in Middle Eastern butchers and are usually cheap.

SERVES 4 AS A TAPA

FOR THE SPICY TOMATO SAUCE
500ml tomate frito (see page 18) or passata
1 dessertspoon smoked paprika
½ dessertspoon chilli powder
Maldon salt and freshly ground black pepper

FOR THE OLIVES
40g pitted black Aragón olives
25ml extra virgin olive oil
25ml Pedro Ximénez balsamic vinegar
1 shallot, peeled and finely diced

FOR THE BRAINS
1 litre oil for deep-frying
2 free-range eggs
a pinch of saffron
100g breadcrumbs
4 milk-fed lamb's brains or 2 normal lamb's brains, sinews removed

Put the tomate frito, paprika and chilli into a pan over a low heat, bring to the boil, then lower the heat and simmer until the sauce has reduced by about two-thirds and is very thick. Season with salt and pepper and set aside.

Roughly chop the olives and put them into a small bowl. Add the olive oil, balsamic vinegar and shallot, mix well and set aside.

Heat the deep-frying oil to 180°C in a large pan or a deep-fryer. Beat the eggs with the saffron and put the breadcrumbs on a plate. Slice the brains in half lengthways. Dip them first into the beaten egg, then into the breadcrumbs, and deep-fry for 3 to 4 minutes, until they are a deep golden brown. Drain on kitchen paper and season well with salt and pepper.

Spoon a goodish amount of spicy tomato sauce on to each serving plate. Put the fried brains on top and finish with a little spoonful of black olives.

MILK-FED LAMB'S KIDNEYS WITH ONIONS AND FENNEL

There are two secrets to remember when contemplating kidneys: make sure the kidneys are brilliantly fresh and be sure not to overcook them, keeping them pink in the middle. The fennel does a great job of cutting through the richness of the kidneys and is key to the success of this dish.

SERVES 4 AS A MAIN

150ml good-quality olive oil
2 very large onions, peeled and finely sliced
2 bay leaves, fresh if possible
100ml brandy
4 thick slices of sourdough bread
2 garlic cloves, peeled
½ a fennel bulb, finely chopped
25ml extra virgin olive oil
25ml Moscatel vinegar
4 fresh mint leaves, cut into fine strips
Maldon salt and freshly ground black pepper
8 lamb's kidneys, sliced in half lengthways, sinews removed
plain flour, for dusting

Heat 100ml of olive oil over a medium heat in a large sauté pan or heavy-bottomed frying pan. Add the onions and bay leaves and cook gently for 35 to 40 minutes, stirring regularly. Pour the brandy into the pan and swirl it round to burn off the alcohol, stirring well. Remove from the heat and set aside.

In a separate frying pan heat 3 dessertspoons of olive oil and lightly colour the sourdough slices until golden on each side. Remove them from the pan and set aside, but don't wash the pan. Cut one of the garlic cloves in half and rub it over one side of the toast.

Finely slice the remaining garlic clove and put into a small bowl with the fennel, the extra virgin olive oil, Moscatel vinegar and mint. Mix well, then season with salt and pepper and set aside.

Add 4 dessertspoons of olive oil to the pan you used for the toast and heat until almost smoking. Dust the kidneys in the flour and shake off any excess, then add to the pan and sauté for 2 minutes on each side.

Put a slice of sourdough toast on each serving plate and spread the onions on top. Divide the kidneys between the toasts and drizzle the fennel dressing over the top. Season with salt and pepper and serve.

CALVES' LIVER WITH CELERIAC PURÉE AND CARAMELIZED ONIONS

The smooth and silky celeriac purée is one of the best accompaniments to calves' liver ever. Make sure the liver you buy is nice and fresh – it should look a vibrant red colour, rather than dull and earthy. And make very sure that you do not overcook it – grey, school-dinner liver will not have your dining companions clamouring for more.

SERVES 4 AS A MAIN

8 tablespoons olive oil
2 large onions, peeled and sliced into thin half-moons
salt and freshly ground black pepper
1 recipe quantity of Celeriac Purée (see page 198)
4 x 180g slices of calves' liver, about 2cm thick
20g plain flour
50ml Veal Stock (see page 213)

Heat 4 tablespoons of olive oil in a heavy-bottomed pan and fry the onions over a medium heat until dark and caramelized, taking care not to burn them. Season with salt and pepper and set aside.

Put the celeriac purée into a small pan and leave to warm through over a very low heat, stirring often.

Heat the remaining 4 tablespoons of olive oil in a large, heavy-bottomed frying pan until beginning to smoke. Dust the liver with the flour and shake off the excess, then sauté for about 2 minutes on each side, seasoning with salt and pepper.

Add the veal stock and remove from the heat, turning the liver once or twice to coat it with the stock as it reduces. Serve the liver with the caramelized onions and celeriac purée.

Tuna Tartar £4.60
Sardines a la Plancha £3.00
Octopus with Capers £2.50
Gambas al Ajillo £2.00
Chipirones £3.50
Mojama with Yellow Pomegranate £3.75
£2.90
£2.00

£8.90
£7.50
£6.60
£7.70

12.50
18.00
6.70
7.50
.80
.80

Tortilla

Classic Tortilla

Prawn and Piquillo Pepper Tortilla   £6.70

Jamón and Spinach Tortilla   £6.70

TORTILLA

We have always been extremely proud of our tortillas, and over the years have experimented with a variety of different ingredients besides the staples: egg, potato and onion. Once you have perfected the simple Classic Tortilla, the world is your 'ostra', as almost any leftovers can be incorporated. Don't skimp on the quality of the eggs – a really good-quality egg like Clarence Court's Burford Brown will make all the difference to how your tortilla tastes. If kept in a cool place, a tortilla is also delicious eaten next day.

CLASSIC TORTILLA

The Spanish save their frying oil carefully in large sealed glass jars for another day. As long as the oil is clean this is a good idea. A mandolin, if you have one, is best for slicing the potatoes.

SERVES 4 AS A TAPA OR LIGHT LUNCH

650ml vegetable oil
750g potatoes, peeled and sliced into 0.5cm rounds
600g onions, peeled and sliced into very thin half-moons
6 free-range eggs (the best quality you can buy)
Maldon salt and freshly ground black pepper
1–2 tablespoons olive oil

Heat the vegetable oil in a large, heavy-bottomed pan until it is just beginning to smoke. Add the potatoes and onions and fry, stirring often, for about 15 minutes, until golden brown. Remove the pan from the heat and leave to cool a little, then take the potatoes and onions out of the oil with a slotted spoon and drain on kitchen paper.

Beat the eggs in a large mixing bowl. Add the potatoes and onions and season well with salt and pepper.

Heat a little olive oil in a 20cm diameter frying pan, preferably non-stick. Add the egg mixture and cook over a medium heat until it is just beginning to set – about 5 minutes. Place a large plate over the frying pan and carefully tip both plate and pan over so that the tortilla ends up on the plate, cooked side up. Slide the tortilla back into the pan and cook for another 5 minutes.

Repeat the procedure twice more, cooking for another 5 minutes or so on each side. The tortilla should still be a little bit runny in the middle.

JAMÓN AND SPINACH TORTILLA

Although the classic tortilla is one of our favourites, when we make it at home we also love using leftover bits and pieces from the fridge. Needless to say, at Barrafina we don't use leftovers but fantastic best-quality Serrano ham from Señor Joselito (from Ham Lovers, see p. 245) and Secretts Farm's finest fresh spinach. This tortilla makes a delicious lunch, served with a crunchy green salad and a slice of crusty bread.

SERVES 4 AS A TAPA OR LIGHT LUNCH

650ml vegetable oil
750g potatoes, peeled and sliced into 0.5cm rounds
600g onions, peeled and sliced into very thin half-moons
1–2 tablespoons olive oil
300g spinach, washed
150g best-quality Serrano ham, cut into 1cm strips
6 free-range eggs (the best quality you can buy)
Maldon salt and freshly ground black pepper

Heat the vegetable oil in a large, heavy-bottomed pan until it is just beginning to smoke. Add the potatoes and onions and fry, stirring often, for about 15 minutes, until golden brown. Remove the pan from the heat and leave to cool a little, then take the potatoes and onions out of the oil with a slotted spoon and drain on kitchen paper.

Drizzle 1 tablespoon of olive oil into a sauté pan or a heavy-bottomed frying pan and place over a medium heat. Add the spinach and cook gently until soft, turning occasionally. Remove to a colander and set aside to drain.

Put the ham into another sauté pan or heavy-bottomed frying pan over a medium heat and cook gently for 30 seconds, until the fat just starts to melt. Remove from the pan and set aside.

Beat the eggs in a large mixing bowl. Add the potatoes, onions, spinach and ham and season well with salt and pepper.

Heat a little more olive oil in a 20cm diameter frying pan, preferably non-stick. Add the egg mixture and cook over a medium heat until it is just beginning to set – about 5 minutes. Place a large plate over the frying pan and carefully tip both plate and pan over so that the tortilla ends up on the plate, cooked side up. Slide the tortilla back into the pan and cook for another 5 minutes.

Repeat the procedure twice more, cooking for about another 5 minutes on each side. The tortilla should still be a little bit runny in the middle.

MORCILLA TORTILLA

This is a rich and satisfying tortilla that is given a bit of extra kick with the addition of some Spanish blood sausage or morcilla, guaranteed to set you up for a tough day or night.

SERVES 4 AS A TAPA OR LIGHT LUNCH

650ml vegetable oil
750g potatoes, peeled and sliced into 0.5cm rounds
600g onions, peeled and sliced into very thin half-moons
1–2 tablespoons olive oil
200g morcilla de Burgos, (see page 43), skin removed
6 free-range eggs (the best quality you can buy)
Maldon salt and freshly ground black pepper

Heat the vegetable oil in a large, heavy-bottomed pan until it is just beginning to smoke. Add the potatoes and onions and fry, stirring often, for about 15 minutes, until golden brown. Remove the pan from the heat and leave to cool a little, then take the potatoes and onions out of the oil with a slotted spoon and drain on kitchen paper.

Heat 1 tablespoon of olive oil in a sauté pan or a heavy-bottomed frying pan and crumble in the morcilla. Stir for a few minutes, then remove the morcilla with a slotted spoon and set aside.

Beat the eggs in a large mixing bowl. Add the potatoes, onions and morcilla and season well with salt and pepper.

Heat a little more olive oil in a 20cm diameter frying pan, preferably non-stick. Add the egg mixture and cook over a medium heat until it is just beginning to set – about 5 minutes. Place a large plate over the frying pan and carefully tip both plate and pan over so that the tortilla ends up on the plate, cooked side up. Slide the tortilla back into the pan and cook for another 5 minutes.

Repeat the procedure twice more, cooking for about another 5 minutes on each side. The tortilla should still be a little bit runny in the middle.

PRAWN AND PIQUILLO TORTILLA

The juicy chunks of prawn and the sweetness of the piquillo peppers make this tortilla a perennial Barrafina favourite.

SERVES 4 AS A TAPA OR LIGHT LUNCH

650ml vegetable oil
750g potatoes, peeled and sliced into 0.5cm rounds
600g onions, peeled and finely sliced
1–2 tablespoons olive oil
16 fresh peeled prawns, cut into 1cm cubes
6 free-range eggs (the best quality you can buy)
200g tinned or jarred piquillo peppers, drained and cut into 0.5cm strips
1 tablespoon finely chopped fresh chives
Maldon salt and freshly ground black pepper

Heat the vegetable oil in a large, heavy-bottomed pan until it is just beginning to smoke. Add the potatoes and onions and fry, stirring often, for about 15 minutes, until golden brown. Remove the pan from the heat and leave to cool a little, then take the potatoes and onions out of the oil with a slotted spoon and drain on kitchen paper.

Heat 1 tablespoon of olive oil over a medium heat in a sauté pan. Add the prawns and cook for 20 to 30 seconds, turning them over in the pan, then remove and set aside.

Beat the eggs in a large mixing bowl. Add the potatoes, onions, prawns, piquillo peppers and chives, and season well with salt and pepper.

Heat a little more olive oil in a 20cm diameter frying pan, preferably non-stick. Add the egg mixture and cook over a medium heat until it is just beginning to set – about 5 minutes. Place a large plate over the frying pan and carefully tip both plate and pan over so that the tortilla ends up on the plate, cooked side up. Slide the tortilla back into the pan and cook for another 5 minutes.

Repeat the procedure twice more, cooking for about another 5 minutes on each side. The tortilla should still be a little bit runny in the middle.

SALADS
AND
VEGETABLES

The Spanish have a reputation for not eating up their healthy greens, but if you venture out into rural Spain you will see that they are even more enthusiastic about their greens than we are in the UK. Salads or vegetables are often eaten on their own as a separate course – runner beans with a little chopped jamón, or baby gem lettuces draped with a few anchovies and a sliver or two of smoked pancetta.

Go to any village in Spain and you will see little allotments on all sides, planted to bursting with fruit and vegetables. Where we have our house, on the north-west coast of Mallorca, the plots are full of fantastic tomatoes, onions, green beans, aubergines, peppers, citrus fruit, peaches, plums, almonds, figs – the list goes on and on.

Like everything else, the quality of the vegetables you use will make an enormous difference: freshness is vital. The vegetables you get in the supermarket are usually several weeks old before they even arrive in store. The older we get, the more we look forward to the prime British vegetable season, the highlight of which is being let loose in our parents' veggie patch in Rutland. Nothing beats seasonal veg straight out of the ground.

At Barrafina we get most of our vegetables from Secretts Farm near Guildford. Hardly the picturesque north coast of Mallorca, where the olive groves run steeply down to meet the glistening blue Mediterranean. However, Secretts grow seasonal English fruit and vegetables and, most importantly, they are picked the day before they deliver to us.

Find a good greengrocer's and ask them what is in season – they will point you in the right direction.

BABY GEM SALAD WITH ANCHOVY AND PANCETTA

We eat this on a daily basis. It has a very clean and healthy feel to it, but due to the presence of the pancetta and anchovy is also extremely satisfying. It works very nicely as a starter, a light lunch or an accompanying dish to something more substantial.

SERVES 4 AS A TAPA OR LIGHT LUNCH

8 slices of smoked pancetta
1 shallot, peeled and very finely diced
15ml sherry vinegar
15ml extra virgin olive oil
2 teaspoons finely chopped fresh chives
Maldon salt and freshly ground black pepper
4 baby gem lettuces, quartered lengthways
8 top-quality Spanish salted anchovies
a handful of fresh flat-leaf parsley

Heat the grill. When it's hot, grill the pancetta until crisp.

Mix the shallot, vinegar, olive oil and chives in a small bowl and season with salt and pepper.

Arrange the baby gem quarters on a large serving dish and spoon over the dressing. Top with the anchovies, grilled pancetta and parsley and serve with good bread.

BEETROOT SALAD WITH PICOS CHEESE

Nightmarish memories of beetroot from the early years at school have made this fabulous vegetable an even more welcome revelation recently. Plucked straight from the earth, cooked and peeled with love and finally dressed correctly, the beetroot is truly versatile. If you can't find Picos de Europa it can be happily replaced with Roquefort or a similar salty, tangy blue cheese.

SERVES 4 AS A TAPA

600g baby beetroots, red and yellow if you can find them
a handful of table salt
1½ dessertspoons finely chopped fresh tarragon
50ml extra virgin olive oil
25ml Moscatel vinegar
Maldon salt and freshly ground black pepper
50g Picos de Europa cheese

Cut the tops off the beetroots and place the roots in a large pan. Cover with cold water, add the table salt and bring to the boil. Cook until tender. They'll take about 20 to 30 minutes. Remove from the heat, drain and set aside to cool a little.

When the beetroots have cooled sufficiently to handle, peel with your hands and discard the skin. Slice them into 2mm rounds, ideally using a mandolin.

Put the beetroot slices, tarragon, extra virgin olive oil and Moscatel vinegar into a serving bowl and season with salt and pepper. Set aside for 2 minutes.

Crumble the blue cheese on top and serve.

BEETROOT SALAD WITH HAZELNUT DRESSING

This simple salad is easy to prepare and keeps well in the fridge. It also works as an accompaniment to grilled oily fish.

SERVES 4 AS A TAPA

600g baby beetroots, red and yellow if you can find them
a handful of table salt
100g best-quality blanched hazelnuts, roughly chopped
50ml extra virgin olive oil
15ml hazelnut oil
4 dessertspoons finely chopped fresh chives
25ml Moscatel vinegar
Maldon salt and freshly ground black pepper

Cut the tops off the beetroots and place the roots in a large pan. Cover with cold water, add the table salt and bring to the boil. Cook until tender. They'll take about 20 to 30 minutes. Remove from the heat, drain and set aside to cool a little.

When the beetroots have cooled sufficiently to handle, peel with your hands and discard the skin. Slice them into 2mm rounds, ideally using a mandolin.

Put the chopped hazelnuts and olive oil into a large bowl and mix well. Add the hazelnut oil, chives and vinegar and mix well. Season with salt and pepper.

Arrange the beetroot on a plate, pour over the dressing, covering all the slices well, and serve.

HERITAGE TOMATO SALAD

The point of this dish is to combine a different assortment of Heritage tomatoes for a brilliant combination of colour, flavour and texture. We usually make this salad with a large, soft, ripe red, a small, more perfumed red, a harder, slighter crunchy green, and a mid-sized yellow. Although one type of really good tomato would make a fine-tasting dish, it would lack the aesthetic appeal of the more eclectic selection. A good greengrocer will help you find Heritage tomatoes – although in the UK you will only find them from June to September. Tomatoes are best served at room temperature rather than straight out of the fridge.

SERVES 4 AS A SIDE

4 tablespoons extra virgin olive oil
2 tablespoons best-quality sherry vinegar
Maldon salt and freshly ground black pepper
2 tablespoons fresh baby basil leaves (or large ones, cut into thin strips)
700g Heritage tomatoes or other best-quality tomatoes, cut into 1cm slices

Put the olive oil, vinegar, salt and pepper into a bowl and whisk. Add the basil and mix well.

Put the tomatoes into a serving bowl, pour the dressing over and serve.

MOJAMA, CHICORY AND POMEGRANATE SALAD

Mojama (wind-dried tuna) has a wonderfully savoury taste and works very well in this simple salad. Having found a delicatessen that supplies mojama, you can keep a supply in the fridge and quietly work your way through it.

SERVES 4 AS A TAPA

1 whole pomegranate
3 dessertspoons Moscatel vinegar
9 dessertspoons extra virgin olive oil
Maldon salt and freshly
ground black pepper
100g mojama (see page 18)
2 heads of chicory

Cut the pomegranate in half crossways. Remove the seeds from one half and put into a bowl. Squeeze the juice of the second half over the seeds in the bowl. Add 1 dessertspoon of Moscatel vinegar and 2 dessertspoons of olive oil, season with salt and pepper, mix well and set aside.

With your very sharpest knife, slice the mojama wafer-thin. Put it into a small bowl and drizzle over 3 dessertspoons of olive oil.

Trim the base from the chicory heads and separate the leaves. Put 4 dessertspoons of oil and 2 dessertspoons of vinegar into a bowl, season with salt and pepper and mix well. Add the chicory leaves and turn them over carefully to coat them with the dressing.

To serve, lay the chicory nicely on a flat serving plate. Spoon over the pomegranate seeds and juice and arrange the mojama on top.

ress

ail Eggs
t with Al-i-oli

teak, Piquillo Peppers,

Chicken Wings, Garlic,
Chilli

Cutlets with Parsnip

per Tortilla

illa

2.5% will be added
at 17.5

WHITE ASPARAGUS WITH ROMESCO SAUCE

The Spanish have an affinity with white asparagus spears that we in the UK have not quite caught on to. Cooked from fresh and handled correctly, they are every bit as worthy as their green cousins, and what better way to serve them than with a truly Catalan Romesco sauce. White asparagus from a tin works quite well if you can't find any fresh – just brown the spears in a little olive oil before serving.

SERVES 4 AS A TAPA

60g flaked almonds
600g white asparagus spears
Maldon salt and freshly ground black pepper
½ recipe quantity of Romesco Sauce (see page 214)
a little extra virgin olive oil

Preheat the oven to 180°C/350°F/gas 4. Put the almonds on a baking tray and toast them in the oven for 2 minutes, until lightly browned.

Peel the asparagus very carefully with a vegetable peeler, removing all the skin. Trim the stalks about 1cm from the bottom.

Bring a large pan of salted water to the boil. Add the asparagus, reduce to a simmer and cook for 20 to 30 minutes, until the asparagus is very tender and soft to the touch. Remove it with a slotted spoon and plunge it into iced water. Drain well and leave to dry on a clean tea towel.

You can serve the asparagus either cold or gently browned in a frying pan with a little olive oil. Whichever way you choose, season it with a little salt and pepper and plenty of romesco sauce, sprinkling over the toasted almonds and a little extra virgin olive oil.

ASPARAGUS WITH PAYOYO CHEESE AND PEDRO XIMÉNEZ BALSAMIC VINEGAR

Payoyo cheese is a cured ewe's milk cheese from Cádiz in the south of Spain and is similar in style to an aged Manchego, which would work just as well here. The cheese's natural saltiness is offset by the sweet complexity of the Pedro Ximénez reduction.

SERVES 4 AS A TAPA

200ml Pedro Ximénez balsamic vinegar
salt and freshly ground black pepper
500g green asparagus,
bottoms cut off the stalks
2 tablespoons olive oil
40g Payoyo cheese
2 or 3 fresh basil leaves,
finely chopped

Put the Pedro Ximénez balsamic vinegar into a small pan over a medium heat and simmer until it has reduced by two-thirds and is sweet and syrupy. Set it aside to cool.

Bring a large pan of salted water to the boil. Add the asparagus and cook until tender – about 2 minutes. Remove it with a slotted spoon and plunge it into iced water. Drain well and leave to dry on a clean tea towel.

Heat the oil in a large, heavy-bottomed pan until just beginning to smoke. Add the asparagus and gently colour on all sides, seasoning with salt and pepper as you go.

To serve, drizzle each serving plate with a little of the Pedro Ximénez reduction and lay the asparagus on top. Using a vegetable peeler, shave the Payoyo over the asparagus and sprinkle with the chopped basil.

BABY ARTICHOKES WITH JAMÓN

The small purple artichokes that arrive in the markets in early summer are perfect for this dish, as they tend to be the sweetest and most tender. This is a hearty dish with robust flavours that could easily, if combined with good bread, be substantial enough for a light lunch.

SERVES 4 AS A TAPA

200ml Chicken Stock (see page 208)
215ml good-quality olive oil
12 Confit Artichokes (see page 217)
Maldon salt and freshly ground black pepper
2 or 3 large shallots, peeled and finely chopped
3 garlic cloves, peeled and finely sliced
100g best-quality Serrano or Jabugo ham, cut into 1cm strips
2 dessertspoons finely chopped fresh flat-leaf parsley

Put the stock into a small pan and heat gently. Keep warm.

Heat the olive oil in a large sauté pan or heavy-bottomed frying pan over a medium heat until it almost starts to smoke. Add the artichokes, season them with salt and pepper and cook for about 3 minutes, until they begin to turn golden brown.

Turn the artichokes over and add the shallots and garlic. Cook until the shallots become translucent and the garlic starts to colour, moving the artichokes around occasionally. Add the ham and cook for a further 2 minutes. Add the warm stock, bring to the boil and cook for a further 5 to 6 minutes, until there are only a few spoonfuls of sauce left.

Put the artichokes into a serving dish, sprinkle the parsley on top and serve immediately.

CRISP FRIED BABY ARTICHOKES WITH ALIOLI

The baby artichokes that are found in spring and early summer are best for this recipe, as they can be fried whole without having to be trimmed too much. Larger artichokes can be used, but these would have to be split lengthways and the choke removed. This dish is excellent as a starter, and a real treat as a nibble to go with drinks at sunset. As with all fried food, eat these good and hot.

SERVES 4 AS A TAPA

1 litre good-quality olive oil
12 Confit Artichokes (see page 217)
60g special flour for frying (see page 17)
Maldon salt and freshly ground black pepper
80ml Alioli (see page 207)
a pinch of smoked paprika
1 dessertspoon finely chopped fresh flat-leaf parsley

Heat the oil to 180°C in a large pan or a deep-fryer. Dust the artichokes generously with the flour, then carefully lower them into the oil and fry for 1½ to 2 minutes, or until golden brown. Drain on kitchen paper and season with salt and pepper.

Put the alioli into a small bowl and sprinkle with paprika. Scatter the parsley over the artichokes and serve straight away, with the alioli.

CALÇOTS WITH ROMESCO SAUCE

In Catalunya between March and April thousands of people can be seen coming together for Calcotades, festivals celebrating the calçot, a cross between a baby leek and a large spring onion. Romesco is a brilliantly versatile sauce – you can use it with fish, poultry or, as in this case, vegetables. You may be able to buy calçots online (see page 244), but if you can't find them you can use large spring onions instead.

SERVES 4 AS A TAPA

2 or 3 bunches of calçots or large spring onions
Maldon salt and freshly ground black pepper
½ recipe quantity of Romesco Sauce (see page 214)
1 tablespoon olive oil
20g toasted flaked almonds, chopped

Trim any roots from the bottoms of the calçots and carefully peel off the outer layer of the leaves. Bring a large pan of salted water to the boil, throw in the calçots and cook for 2 minutes. While they are cooking, prepare a bowl of iced water. After 2 minutes, remove the calçots with a slotted spoon and plunge them into the iced water. Drain well and place on a clean tea towel to dry.

Put the romesco sauce into a small pan and reheat gently.

Heat the olive oil in a large, heavy-bottomed frying pan until just beginning to smoke. Add the calçots and fry gently on each side until nicely browned, seasoning with salt and pepper as you go.

Serve the calçots with the romesco sauce and sprinkled with the toasted nuts.

CHICKPEAS, SPINACH AND PANCETTA

When we opened our first restaurant, Fino, we had this Catalan classic on the menu and it has remained there and at Barrafina ever since. It is a rustic, peasanty sort of dish that is very soothing and contains everything you could need for a light meal. Make sure the chickpeas are cooked until they are very tender so they absorb all the flavours.

SERVES 4 AS A LIGHT MAIN

240g dried chickpeas, soaked in water overnight and drained
4 bay leaves, fresh if possible
1 large onion, peeled and cut in half
12 tablespoons extra virgin olive oil, plus extra for drizzling
240g smoked pancetta, cut into 1cm lardons
1 large shallot, peeled and finely chopped
6 garlic cloves, peeled and finely chopped
500ml Chicken Stock (see page 208)
300g baby spinach leaves
Maldon salt and freshly ground black pepper

Put the drained chickpeas into a large pan with the bay leaves, onion and plenty of water. Bring to the boil, then cook for 45 minutes or until the chickpeas are tender. Drain the chickpeas, discarding the bay leaves and onion, and set aside to cool.

Heat the olive oil in a large sauté pan or heavy-bottomed frying pan over a high heat until almost smoking. Add the pancetta and cook until it starts to caramelize. Add the shallots and garlic and cook gently for 2 minutes.

Add the chicken stock to the pan and simmer until it has reduced by half. Add the chickpeas, reduce the heat and simmer for 4 to 5 minutes. Add the spinach and cook for a further 30 seconds, folding the leaves in gently.

Drizzle with a little olive oil and season with salt and pepper if necessary. Serve with crusty sourdough bread.

COURGETTE FLOWERS WITH CHANTERELLES, PRAWNS AND A SPICY TOMATO SAUCE

Courgette flowers are available in the UK from June to September, and when stuffed with something tasty and crisply fried are really delicious. Here we stuff them with a mixture of prawns and chanterelles, which are conveniently in season during more or less the same period as the courgettes.

SERVES 4 AS A TAPA

50ml olive oil
100g chanterelle mushrooms, cleaned
50g raw prawns, peeled and chopped
1 shallot, peeled and finely chopped
2 garlic cloves, peeled and finely chopped
1 tablespoon fresh thyme leaves
2 tablespoons chopped fresh flat-leaf parsley
Maldon salt and freshly ground black pepper
1 litre oil for deep-frying
8 courgette flowers

FOR THE SPICY TOMATO SAUCE
250ml tomate frito (see page 18) or passata
1 dessertspoon smoked paprika
½ dessertspoon chilli powder

FOR THE TEMPURA
150g cornflour
150g plain flour
300ml sparkling water

Heat the olive oil in a heavy-bottomed frying pan and fry the chanterelles until they have given up any water and are nicely brown. Add the prawns and cook for another 2 minutes. Add the shallots, garlic and thyme and cook for 2 minutes more, then add the parsley, season with salt and leave to cool.

To make the tomato sauce, put the tomate frito, paprika and chilli into a pan and simmer until reduced by two-thirds and very thick. Season and set aside.

Heat the oil for deep-frying to 180°C in a large pan or a deep-fryer.

Remove the stamens delicately from the courgette flowers, taking great care not to rip the petals. Spoon into the cavity of each flower enough of the mushroom and prawn mixture to fill it, and gently wrap the top of the flower around to make a seal.

To make the tempura batter, mix the cornflour and plain flour in a large mixing bowl and whisk in the water bit by bit. Keep whisking until the mixture is silky smooth. Season with a little freshly ground black pepper. Coat each courgette flower with the batter and deep-fry for 2 to 3 minutes, making sure the flowers do not stick to the bottom of the pan. Remove on to kitchen paper to drain.

Serve the stuffed courgette flowers with a good spoonful of the spicy tomato sauce.

Vegetables

HISPI CABBAGE WITH PANCETTA

Hispi cabbage is the pointy green one with tight, bright leaves. This dish works just as well with all the other brassicas, should you wish to mix them up. Believe it or not, this is what our father eats for weeks on end when he is on his annual diet, albeit with less olive oil and only a half portion of lardons.

SERVES 4 AS A SIDE OR DIETARY DINNER

Maldon salt and freshly ground black pepper
2 Hispi or Savoy cabbages, core removed, heart finely sliced
200ml extra virgin olive oil
120g smoked pancetta, cut into lardons
2 garlic cloves, peeled and finely chopped

Bring a large pan of salted water to the boil. Add the cabbage and blanch for 30 seconds, then drain and plunge it directly into ice-cold water. Drain the cabbage again, then spread the leaves on a tea towel and set aside.

Heat the olive oil in a large sauté pan or heavy-bottomed frying pan over a medium heat. When the oil is almost smoking, add the pancetta lardons and fry for 3 to 4 minutes, stirring occasionally, until caramelized and crisp. Add the cabbage and toss well with the pancetta and oil for 2 or 3 minutes.

Add the finely chopped garlic, mix well and cook for a further 2 minutes. Season to taste with salt and pepper and serve straight away.

GRILLED AUBERGINES WITH CRISP FRIED COURGETTES

This is a fun mix of the same marinade used with two different vegetables, cooked in two different ways. If you can't get hold of a white aubergine, use two black ones.

SERVES 4 AS A TAPA

600ml olive oil
20 garlic cloves, peeled and flattened with the back of a knife
8 bay leaves, fresh if possible
a bunch of fresh thyme
1 tablespoon cayenne pepper
2 tablespoons paprika
Maldon salt and freshly ground black pepper
1 white aubergine, sliced into 1cm rounds
1 black aubergine, sliced into 1cm rounds
150g green courgettes, sliced into 1cm rounds
150g yellow courgettes, sliced into 1cm rounds
1 litre oil for deep-frying
100g plain flour
3 free-range eggs
4 tablespoons honey

Turn the oven to its lowest temperature. In a large bowl combine the olive oil, garlic, bay leaves, thyme, cayenne, paprika, salt and pepper and mix well. Divide this mixture equally between 2 bowls. Add the aubergines to one bowl and the courgettes to the other. Mix well and leave to marinate for 2 hours.

Heat the oil for deep-frying to 180°C in a large pan or a deep-fryer. Heat a large, heavy-bottomed frying pan.

Spread the flour on a plate and beat the eggs in a bowl. Remove the courgettes from the marinade. Dip them first into the flour, then into the beaten eggs, and deep-fry in the hot oil for 2 to 3 minutes, or until golden brown. Remove from the oil on to kitchen paper, season with salt and pepper and keep warm in the oven – you will probably have to cook the courgettes in batches.

While the courgettes are frying, remove the aubergines from the marinade. When the courgettes are ready, fry the aubergines in the hot frying pan for 2 to 3 minutes on each side, or until cooked. You won't need any more oil, as the aubergines will retain quite a lot from the marinade. Again you may have to cook them in batches – keep any cooked aubergines warm in the oven while you finish the rest. Remove from the pan and season with salt and pepper.

Serve the aubergines and courgettes together in a serving dish, drizzled with the honey.

PAPAS A LO POBRE

Literally 'poor man's potatoes', these nonetheless make an excellent accompaniment to both fish and meat. Their simplicity in fact can be considered a benefit when combined with a robust-flavoured partner, as it tends not to interfere.

SERVES 4 TO 6 AS A SIDE

700g potatoes, sliced into 0.5cm rounds
a small bunch of fresh thyme
5 bay leaves, fresh if possible
1 very large white onion, peeled and sliced into 0.5cm half-moons
2 whole heads of garlic, halved horizontally
4 tablespoons extra virgin olive oil
Maldon salt and freshly ground black pepper

Preheat the oven to 180°C/350°F/gas 4. Line an oven dish or roasting tray with baking parchment and tip in all the ingredients. Mix well and roast in the oven for about 50 minutes, until the potatoes are lightly browned and cooked through.

Remove the garlic and thyme and serve at once.

CELERIAC PURÉE

Celeriac always reminds us of the wise and ancient proverb 'Do not judge a book by its cover'. An ugly brute, it has such a wonderful flavour and is often a welcome break from potatoes. You can use milk instead of cream if you like, or a combination of the two.

SERVES 4 TO 6 AS A SIDE

½ a large celeriac (about 500g), peeled and cut into 3cm cubes
2 bay leaves, fresh if possible
400ml double cream
40g butter
50ml olive oil
Maldon salt

Put the celeriac, bay leaves, cream, butter and olive oil into a large pan and add plenty of salt. Bring to the boil, then reduce the heat and simmer for 25 minutes.

Remove from the heat and with a slotted spoon transfer the celeriac and 1 bay leaf into a blender or food processor, discarding the liquid left behind. Blitz well to make a smooth purée.

Adjust the seasoning if necessary and serve.

PISTO AND DUCK EGG

This is a great vegetarian main course that is perfect for the days when neither fish nor meat holds any appeal. Pisto has nothing to do with pesto, but is similar in style to the French ratatouille. Don't rush the cooking of the vegetables, as it is really important to caramelize them properly.

SERVES 6 AS A MAIN

220ml extra virgin olive oil
6 garlic cloves, peeled and finely sliced
1 red onion, peeled and cut into 2cm dice
1 large white onion, peeled and cut into 2cm dice
2 aubergines, cut into 2cm dice
2 green peppers, seeded and cut into 2cm dice
2 red peppers, seeded and cut into 2cm dice
2 large courgettes, cut into 2cm dice
4 teaspoons sweet smoked paprika
4 bay leaves, fresh if possible
6 tomatoes, cut into 2cm dice
6 fresh duck eggs

Heat 100ml of olive oil in a large casserole or pan over a medium heat. Add the garlic and cook gently until lightly golden. Add the onions and cook for 10 minutes, stirring occasionally, until soft. Add the aubergines and peppers, cook for 2 minutes, then add the courgettes and another 60ml of olive oil and cook for a further 3 minutes.

Now add the paprika, bay leaves and a further 30ml of olive oil and cook for 10 to 15 minutes, stirring occasionally. Add the tomatoes, cook for 5 minutes and add another 30ml of olive oil. Cook for 5 minutes more, then remove from the heat.

Heat a little more olive oil in a small pan and fry the duck eggs one at a time. Spoon the pisto on to serving plates, put the fried eggs on top, and serve with crusty sourdough bread.

SPINACH, PINENUT AND RAISIN COCA

A Mallorquín classic, this is a great dish that you can serve as part of a lunchtime spread or take on a picnic. You can use any manzanilla or fino sherry, but having researched for many years, La Gitana is our favourite.

SERVES 8 AS A TAPA

FOR THE DOUGH
400g plain flour, plus extra for dusting
1 teaspoon salt
200ml water
3 tablespoons of manzanilla or fino sherry (e.g. La Gitana)
3 tablespoons extra virgin olive oil, plus extra for the tray
22g fresh yeast or 1 tablespoon dried yeast, dissolved in 1 tablespoon warm water

FOR THE TOPPING
4 tablespoons extra virgin olive oil, plus extra for drizzling
4 large onions, peeled and roughly chopped
1 tablespoon smoked paprika, plus 1 teaspoon
1 tablespoon cumin seeds
50g pinenuts
50g raisins, soaked in 75ml sherry vinegar for 2 hours
500g baby spinach
Maldon salt and freshly ground black pepper

Put the flour and salt into a large mixing bowl. Add the water, sherry, olive oil and the yeast mixture and stir well. If the mixture is too wet to handle, add a dusting of plain flour and work thoroughly with your hands until well mixed. Put the dough into a clean bowl, cover with a damp cloth and leave somewhere warm for 15 to 20 minutes to allow it to rise.

Preheat the oven to 180°C/350°F/gas 4. Dust a work surface with plain flour and roll out the dough thinly to a rectangular shape about 2 to 3mm thick. Rub a baking tray about 40 x 30cm with olive oil, then place the dough carefully on it and prick it all over with a fork.

Heat 2 tablespoons of olive oil in a large sauté pan or heavy-bottomed frying pan over a medium heat and cook the onions gently for 5 to 10 minutes, until soft and translucent. Add the tablespoon of paprika and the cumin seeds and mix well. Leave to cool a little, then spread the onions evenly over the coca base, leaving a 1.5cm gap around the edge. Bake in the oven for 25 to 30 minutes, or until the pastry turns golden.

Heat another 2 tablespoons of olive oil in a large sauté pan or heavy-bottomed frying pan over a medium heat and colour the pinenuts until golden brown. Squeeze the excess vinegar out of the raisins and add to the pan with the teaspoon of paprika and the spinach. Season with salt and pepper and cook for 1 to 2 minutes, stirring, until the spinach starts to wilt. Spread the spinach over the coca, drizzle with a little olive oil and serve.

SAUCES, STOCKS AND BASICS

Sauces and stocks are an essential part of any cook's repertoire. The professional chef is lucky enough to have all types of stocks and sauces at hand, ready to be used at a moment's notice, but at home stocks take time to produce and require organization on the part of the cook. Make stocks in large quantities and freeze what you have left over in small amounts. Fishmongers, butchers and supermarkets are beginning to make half-decent stocks which you can use if you are short of time or energy – these won't give the same richness and flavour as homemade stocks but will often be good enough.

PEDRO XIMÉNEZ REDUCTION

Pedro Ximénez is famed for making very sweet dessert-style sherry, mostly used for pouring over ice cream. However, they also make an excellent, dark, rich balsamic vinegar. Here we reduce it by two-thirds to make a concentrated syrup that makes an excellent addition to all sorts of dishes, giving them greater complexity and depth of flavour.

12 tablespoons Pedro Ximénez balsamic vinegar

Put the balsamic vinegar into a small pan over a medium heat and simmer until it has reduced by two-thirds and is sweet and syrupy. Set it aside to cool.

AJILLO

Known by Nieves and her team as 'Magic', ajillo gives that perfect lift to so many dishes. It is worthwhile making a goodly batch, as it stores well in the fridge and always comes in handy.

MAKES ABOUT 80ML

75ml extra virgin olive oil
3 garlic cloves, peeled and finely chopped
a small handful of flat-leaf parsley, stalks removed, finely chopped

Put the olive oil into a small bowl and stir in the garlic and parsley.

ALIOLI

Roasting the garlic takes the sting out of the tail and adds sweetness to the alioli. This is such a versatile sauce – it works brilliantly with fish, meat and vegetables or even spread over hot toast.

MAKES ABOUT 300ML

3 whole heads of garlic
250ml extra virgin olive oil
3 free-range egg yolks
juice of ½ a lemon
Maldon salt and freshly
ground black pepper

Preheat the oven to 180°C/350°F/gas 4. Put the heads of garlic on a large sheet of foil and drizzle them with a ltlle olive oil, then wrap the foil up and roast in the oven for 20 to 30 minutes, until completely soft. When cool enough to handle, pop the garlic cloves out of their skins and set aside.

Whiz up the eggs in a blender or food processor, then little by little, with the motor running, add the rest of the olive oil through the funnel to form a thick emulsion.

Throw in the roast garlic and whiz again. Add the lemon juice and season well with salt and pepper.

CHICKEN STOCK

It is always worthwhile having some chicken stock knocking around, as it often comes in handy. It freezes very well, so there is no harm in making double the quantity and freezing some for another day. Supermarkets and butchers are getting much better at selling pre-made stock, which makes a reasonable substitute if you haven't the time or inclination to make your own. Despite what a certain celebrity chef might tell you, don't use stock cubes – they are much too salty.

MAKES 2 LITRES

1kg raw chicken bones
25ml olive oil
2 carrots, peeled and diced
2 leeks, diced
2 sticks of celery, diced
2 shallots, peeled and diced
1 whole head of garlic,
halved horizontally
2 bay leaves, fresh if possible
a small bunch of fresh thyme
a small bunch of fresh flat-leaf parsley

Preheat the oven to 180°C/350°F/gas 4. Put the chicken bones into a roasting tin and roast in the oven for 20 minutes, turning twice.

Heat the olive oil in a large, heavy-bottomed pan. Add the carrots, leeks, celery, shallots, garlic, bay leaves, thyme and parsley and cook slowly until well browned and mushy – about 30 minutes.

Add 4 litres of cold water and the chicken bones. Bring to the boil, then reduce the heat to a gentle simmer and cook for 1½ to 2 hours. Every 10 minutes or so, skim the impurities from the surface of the stock with a large spoon.

Strain the stock through a fine sieve and keep refrigerated or frozen until needed.

BISQUE

We use this bisque quite a lot in our seafood cooking, as it adds a wonderful depth of flavour to the dish. It freezes well, so you can make double or even triple quantities and freeze what you don't need in ice trays. Defrost as much or as little as you need at a time.

MAKES 1.5 LITRES

25ml olive oil
1kg raw prawns, shell on
2 carrots, peeled and diced
1 stick of celery, diced
1 bulb of fennel, diced
1 leek, diced
2 shallots, peeled and diced
1 whole head of garlic, cloves peeled
3 bay leaves, fresh if possible
2 tablespoons tomato purée
200ml brandy

Heat the olive oil in a large, heavy-bottomed pan until smoking. Add the prawns and cook over a medium heat for 15 minutes, mashing and crushing them as you go. Add the carrots, celery, fennel, leeks, shallots, garlic and bay leaves and cook for another 30 minutes, until well browned and mushy.

Add the tomato purée and brandy and ignite to burn off the alcohol. Add 4 litres of water, bring to the boil, then reduce the heat to a simmer and cook for 1 to 1½ hours, until the liquid has reduced by about two-thirds.

Strain a couple of times through a fine sieve and keep refrigerated or frozen until needed.

SQUID INK SAUCE

You can buy squid ink in little sachets from your fishmonger to make this amazing-looking and fantastic-tasting sauce.

MAKES ABOUT 200ML

25ml extra virgin olive oil
2 shallots, peeled and finely diced
3 garlic cloves, peeled and finely sliced
3 bay leaves, fresh if possible
100ml manzanilla sherry
100ml brandy
400ml Bisque (see page 211)
2 sachets of squid ink
Maldon salt and freshly
ground black pepper

Heat the olive oil in a medium pan. Add the shallots, garlic and bay leaves and cook for 8 minutes over a medium heat. Add the manzanilla and brandy and simmer until reduced by half.

Add the bisque and squid ink, season with salt and pepper and cook gently for 15 minutes so that the flavours can infuse. The sauce should be thick enough to coat the back of a spoon. If not, reduce it some more.

Pass the mixture through a fine sieve and use straight away.

VEAL SAUCE

It is always better to make your own stock, but it is possible to buy reasonable versions from butchers and supermarkets nowadays. Just buy 2 litres and start at the beginning of the sauce recipe.

MAKES ABOUT 500ML

FOR THE VEAL STOCK
(makes 2 litres)
3kg veal marrow bones
2 tablespoons honey
25ml olive oil
2 carrots, peeled and diced
2 leeks, diced
2 sticks of celery, diced
2 shallots, peeled and diced
1 whole head of garlic,
halved horizontally
2 bay leaves, fresh if possible
a small bunch of fresh thyme
a small bunch of fresh flat-leaf parsley

FOR THE SAUCE
1 bottle of red wine
2 litres veal stock

First make the veal stock. Preheat the oven to 180°C/350°F/gas 4. Put the veal bones into a roasting tin and roast in the oven for 15 minutes, turning once. Remove from the oven, stir in the honey, mix well and roast for another 5 minutes.

Heat the olive oil in a large, heavy-bottomed pan. Add the carrots, leeks, celery, shallots, garlic, bay leaves, thyme and parsley and cook slowly until well browned and mushy – about 30 minutes. Add the roasted veal bones and pour in 4 litres of water. Bring to the boil, then reduce the heat to a gentle simmer and cook for 1½ to 2 hours. Every 10 minutes or so, skim the impurities from the surface.

Strain the stock through a fine sieve. You should have about 2 litres of liquid.

To make the veal sauce, bring the red wine to the boil in a large pan, then simmer until it has reduced by half. Add the veal stock and continue to simmer until the liquid has reduced by three-quarters and the sauce is thick and glossy.

ROMESCO SAUCE

Romesco sauce is extremely versatile and can accompany fish, meat and vegetable dishes. It comes from Catalunya, and there are many different recipes and variations – this just happens to be ours - but all are based on chillies, peppers, nuts, garlic, tomato and sherry vinegar. Romesco keeps well in the fridge.

MAKES ENOUGH FOR 6–8 GENEROUS PORTIONS (ABOUT 650ML)

1 dried red chilli, soaked in warm water for 2 hours
4 dried choricero peppers (see page 18), soaked in warm water for 2 hours
5 plum tomatoes
100ml olive oil, plus 3 tablespoons
Maldon salt and freshly ground black pepper
1 whole head of garlic, halved horizontally
100g blanched almonds
1 slice of good-quality white bread, about 2cm thick
50ml sherry vinegar

Heat the oven to 180°C/350°F/gas 4. Drain the soaked chilli and choricero peppers, then remove the seeds and set aside.

Put the tomatoes into a roasting dish. Drizzle them with a tablespoon of olive oil and season with salt and pepper. Wrap the two halves of garlic in foil and add to the roasting dish. Roast in the oven for 20 minutes. When cool enough, pop the garlic cloves out of their skins and set aside.

Meanwhile, in a separate smaller roasting dish, toast the almonds in the same oven for 2 to 3 minutes until lightly browned. Be careful – they burn fast!

Heat 2 tablespoons of olive oil in a small frying pan and fry the bread on both sides until golden brown.

Put the chilli, choriceros, roasted tomatoes, garlic, almonds, bread and vinegar into a blender or food processor. Add 100ml of olive oil and blitz until smooth. Season with plenty of salt and pepper and keep in the fridge until needed.

JERUSALEM ARTICHOKE AND JAMÓN PURÉE

This is a delicious accompaniment to scallops, and also works very well with white fish such as sea bass. You could even spoon it over hot toast. We use trimmings from whole legs of Serrano ham, but you could just as easily buy slices – it's just more expensive.

SERVES 6 AS AN ACCOMPANIMENT
TO SCALLOPS OR FISH

600g Jerusalem artichokes
1 litre full-fat milk
1 bay leaf
3 tablespoons olive oil
30g Serrano ham trimmings
2 shallots, peeled and finely diced
1 garlic clove, peeled and chopped
Maldon salt and freshly
ground black pepper
500ml Chicken Stock (see page 208)
50ml extra virgin olive oil
Maldon salt and freshly
ground black pepper

Peel the artichokes and place them in a large pan with the milk and bay leaf. Bring to the boil, then reduce to a simmer and cook for 20 minutes, or until tender. Remove the artichokes with a slotted spoon and set aside.

Heat 3 tablespoons of olive oil in a medium frying pan and gently fry the ham until the fat is just beginning to melt. Add the shallots and garlic and continue to cook until translucent. Add the artichokes, a little salt and pepper and the chicken stock, and cook over a medium heat until the liquid has almost all evaporated. Skim any impurities that rise to the top as you go.

Tip the whole lot into a blender, add the extra virgin olive oil and blitz well. Adjust the seasoning carefully and serve.

CONFIT ARTICHOKES

This is the first step towards making Crisp Fried Artichokes (see page 188) or Baby Artichokes with Jamón (see page 187).

SERVES 4

2kg baby artichokes (about 20)
1.5 litres olive oil
2 carrots, peeled and cut into 1cm dice
1 leek, cut into 1cm dice
2 whole heads of garlic, halved horizontally
a small bunch of fresh thyme
4 bay leaves, fresh if possible

Trim the outer leaves of the baby artichokes, then with a sharp knife thinly peel the stalk and base.

Heat the oil to 80°C in a large pan and add the carrots, leeks, garlic and herbs. Add the artichokes to the pan and cook for 20 to 25 minutes, or until tender.

Drain the artichokes, discarding the other vegetables and herbs, and place them, stalk up, on a wire tray to drain off any excess oil.

DESSERTS

Unlike their northern neighbours the French, the Spanish are not famed for being brilliant pâtissiers. Even top-quality Spanish restaurants will buy in their puddings frozen and might at most make a couple of homemade tarts or a Crema Catalana. We often finish a meal in Spain with some fantastic fresh fruit or some cheese. However, there are moments in life when only a proper pudding will do, and at Barrafina we have created a short list of really good ones. Here goes . . .

CREMA CATALANA

No Spanish cookbook would be complete without a recipe for Crema Catalana. The recipes vary in quality a great deal, and we have to say that we think ours is one of the best. It is suggested that it was first devised not in Spain or indeed France but in Cambridge, where as early as the 1600s Burnt Cambridge Cream was in fashion.

SERVES 4

FOR THE CUSTARD
500ml single cream
zest of ½ a lemon
zest of ½ an orange
1 small stick of cinnamon
3 free-range egg yolks
60g caster sugar

FOR THE CARAMEL TOPPING
110g caster sugar

To make the custard, pour the cream into a pan, add the orange and lemon zests and the cinnamon and heat slowly until it just comes to the boil. Remove from the heat and allow to cool for 5 minutes.

In a heatproof mixing bowl, beat the egg yolks with the caster sugar until pale and thick. Strain the warm cream through a fine sieve on to the egg yolk mixture, whisking constantly. Discard the zests and cinnamon.

Set the bowl over a large pan of gently simmering water (or pour the custard into the top of a bain marie, set over gently simmering water). Stir constantly with a wooden spoon until the custard thickens to the correct consistency. It should be thick enough to thinly coat the back of your spoon. You will need to be patient – this may take as long as half an hour. Remove from the heat and pour into 4 x 175ml ramekins. Allow to cool, then place in the refrigerator for 1 to 2 hours to set.

To make the caramel topping, sprinkle the sugar evenly over the surface of the custards and caramelize with a blowtorch (or under a very hot grill) until the sugar turns a mahogany brown. Chill for 30 minutes before serving.

CHERRY CATALANA

This is a delicious variation on the great classic. Other fruit can be substituted for the cherries.

SERVES 6

185g best black cherries, pitted and cut in half
2 small sticks of cinnamon
2 vanilla pods, split lengthways
140g caster sugar
8 free-range egg yolks
350ml full-fat milk
150ml single cream
1 star anise
1 clove
zest of 1 orange
zest of 1 lemon
6 leaves of fresh mint, finely sliced

FOR THE CARAMEL TOPPING
6 tablespoons caster sugar

Put the cherries into a large pan with 1 stick of cinnamon, 1 vanilla pod and 1 tablespoon of caster sugar, and cook for 20 minutes over a medium heat, stirring occasionally, until the cherries are soft and the juices start to run. Remove and set aside.

In a large mixing bowl, whisk the egg yolks and remaining caster sugar until thick and pale in colour.

Put the milk, cream, star anise, clove, orange and lemon zests and remaining cinnamon and vanilla pod into a large pan over a medium heat. Just before it comes to the boil, remove from the heat and allow to cool for a couple of minutes.

Pour the milk slowly on to the eggs and sugar, whisking constantly. Pass the mixture through a fine sieve, discarding all the flavourings, and then with a large spoon skim the scum from the top until all the white froth has been removed and only the yellow custard remains. Discard the scum, allow the custard to cool and refrigerate overnight.

Preheat the oven to 160°C/300°F/gas 2. Place 6 x 175ml ramekins in a large baking tray. Divide the cherries evenly over the bottom of the pots and pour in the cold custard mixture. Pour cold water into the tray to come about 1cm from the rims of the pots. Put into the oven and cook for 40 to 50 minutes, or until the Catalanas start to become solid. Remove them from the oven, then take them carefully out of the baking tray and allow to cool. Refrigerate for a minimum of 2 hours.

To make the caramel topping, sprinkle the sugar evenly over the surface of each custard and caramelize with a blowtorch (or under a very hot grill) until the sugar turns a mahogany brown. Chill for 30 minutes and serve garnished with the mint.

CHOCOLATE MOUSSE

When helping Nieves with this recipe, we accidentally stirred the melting chocolate . . . Disaster! The chocolate went hard and we had to start again. We were forgiven, but it was an important lesson.

SERVES 4

FOR THE MOUSSE
100g best-quality dark chocolate (70% cocoa solids)
100g best-quality milk chocolate
zest of 1 orange
500ml double cream

FOR THE GANACHE
180g best-quality dark chocolate (70% cocoa solids), broken into small pieces
15g cocoa powder
90ml full-fat milk
150ml single cream
1 tablespoon brandy

FOR THE CRUMBLE
250g plain flour
100g caster sugar
60g cocoa powder
200g unsalted butter, cut into cubes

First make the mousse. Construct a bain-marie by filling a large pan one-third full of water. Bring to a simmer. In a bowl big enough to fit over the pan without its bottom touching the water, place the chocolate and let it melt gently without stirring. Add the orange zest to the melting chocolate (do not stir the chocolate, or it will seize). When the chocolate has melted, remove from the heat and set aside to cool.

Whisk the double cream in a large bowl using an electric whisk until it starts to thicken. Add the cooled chocolate and whisk for 20 seconds, then use a plastic spatula to fold the mixture together carefully and ensure that the chocolate is entirely integrated with the cream. Refrigerate for a minimum of 2 hours.

To make the ganache, put the chocolate pieces and cocoa powder into a large bowl. Heat the milk and cream over a medium heat until almost boiling and slowly pour over the chocolate, stirring well. Add the brandy and stir until silky smooth. Allow to cool, then cover with clingfilm and refrigerate for at least 2 hours.

To make the crumble, preheat the oven to 160°C/300°F/gas 2. Put the flour, sugar and cocoa into a food processor. Add the butter and pulse gradually until you have a crumble consistency. Take the mixture out of the processor and bring it together with your hands to make a dough. Spread evenly over a non-stick baking tray and bake in the oven for 15 to 20 minutes, or until it has a soft biscuit-like texture. Set aside to cool.

To serve, divide the mousse equally between 8 tumblers or glass dishes. Spoon the ganache over the mousse and sprinkle with the biscuit crumble.

CHOCOLATE TART

Rich, crumbly pastry with a dark chocolate filling is the sort of thing that gets us all excited. At Barrafina we serve this tart still warm from the oven.

SERVES 12

FOR THE PASTRY
115g icing sugar
350g plain flour
215g unsalted butter,
cut into small cubes
3 free-range egg yolks
butter, for greasing tart tin
plain flour, for dusting

FOR THE FILLING
375g best-quality dark chocolate
(70% cocoa solids)
250g unsalted butter,
cut into small cubes
75g caster sugar
4 free-range eggs
3 free-range egg yolks

Put the icing sugar and flour into a food processor and start to blend slowly. Add the butter, making sure it is well integrated. Add the egg yolks and pulse until the mixture clumps together. Stop mixing and remove the pastry. Bring it together with your hands – it should have a putty-like texture. Wrap in clingfilm and refrigerate overnight.

Preheat the oven to 200°C/400°F/gas 6. Grease a 30cm tart tin with butter and dust it with flour. Flour a work surface, then roll out the pastry into a large circle 2mm thick and lay it carefully in the tin, leaving the excess pastry overhanging. Prick the base of the pastry all over with a fork. Place the tin on a baking tray, then cut out a large disc of baking parchment just a little larger than the tin and delicately place on top of the pastry. Weight it down with baking beans.

Bake in the oven for 15 to 20 minutes, or until the edges of the pastry start to turn golden. Take out of the oven, remove the baking parchment and beans and allow to cool. Carefully trim any excess pastry from the rim of the tart, leaving the tart tin on the baking tray. Turn the oven down to 160°C/300°F/gas 2.

To make the filling, melt the chocolate and butter gently in a bowl over simmering water until completely smooth, then remove from the heat.

Whisk the sugar, eggs and yolks together until pale and creamy. Carefully add the melted chocolate, folding it in gently with a plastic spatula so as not to lose the lightness of the mixture. When the chocolate has been totally integrated, carefully spoon the mixture into the pastry case, spreading it out evenly.

Bake in the oven for 30 to 40 minutes, and serve.

MACEDONIA

Why the Spanish should call this excellent fruit salad Macedonia, no one can tell us. But they do, so we shall too.

SERVES 4

750ml freshly squeezed orange juice
50ml brandy
2 star anise
2 cloves
2 sticks of cinnamon, broken in half
2 vanilla pods, cut in half lengthways
13 fresh mint leaves
1 Braeburn or similar eating apple, peeled, cored and cut into 0.5cm cubes
1 ripe pear, peeled, cored and cut into 0.5cm cubes
1 ripe peach, stone removed, peeled and cut into 0.5cm cubes
1 ripe mango, stone removed, peeled and cut into 0.5cm cubes

FOR THE VANILLA CREAM
250ml double cream
50g icing sugar, sifted
seeds from 1 vanilla pod

FOR THE CRUMBLE (OPTIONAL)
8 plain digestive biscuits
50g unsalted butter, cut into cubes
1 tablespoon icing sugar

Put the orange juice, brandy, star anise, cloves, cinnamon, vanilla pods and mint leaves into a pan over a medium heat and bring to the boil, then lower the heat and simmer for about 25 minutes, until reduced by half. Strain through a sieve into a separate bowl, discarding the flavourings, then allow to cool and chill in the fridge.

To make the vanilla cream, whip the cream in a bowl with the icing sugar and vanilla seeds until it starts to become firm. Put in the fridge until needed.

To make the crumble, if using, first preheat the oven to 180°C/350°F/gas 4. Line a baking tray with baking parchment and lay the biscuits on top. Scatter over the butter, sift over the icing sugar and bake in the oven for 3 minutes. Remove from the oven, allow to cool, then crumble the mixture with your hands and set aside.

Divide the diced fruit with all its juice between 4 glass tumblers and pour the orange sauce over the top. Spoon a little cream over the fruit, dust with the crumble and serve.

MIL HOJAS

This dessert would be a delicious alternative to a traditional birthday cake. Mil Hojas is the Spanish translation of the French mille feuilles.

SERVES 6

FOR THE CREAM
250ml double cream
50g icing sugar, sifted
seeds from 1 vanilla pod

FOR THE CUSTARD
1 litre full-fat milk
1 stick of cinnamon
1 vanilla pod
zest of 1 lemon
6 free-range egg yolks
200g caster sugar
80g cornflour
500g puff pastry, defrosted if frozen
50g flaked almonds, toasted
icing sugar, for dusting

Whip the cream with the icing sugar and vanilla seeds until it starts to become firm. Spoon into a piping bag fitted with a nozzle and refrigerate.

To make the custard, heat the milk, cinnamon, vanilla pod and lemon zest in a large pan and bring almost to the boil. Remove from the heat, pass through a fine sieve and set aside. Whisk the egg yolks and sugar in a large mixing bowl until pale. Add the cornflour and keep whisking until it is all incorporated, then pour in the milk and mix well. Pour into a clean pan over a very low heat, whisking continuously and not allowing the custard to boil, until it is the consistency of light mayonnaise. Leave to cool, then spoon into a piping bag fitted with a nozzle and put into the fridge to get completely cold.

Roll out the puff pastry on a floured surface to a large rectangle about 2mm thick and measuring 45 x 25cm. Cut this into 3 smaller rectangles measuring 15 x 25cm. Line a large baking tray with baking parchment and lay the pastry sheets on it side by side. Bake for 20 to 25 minutes, until the pastry is golden and risen. Remove from the oven, then take another large baking tray and rest it directly on top of the cooked pastry, gently pressing down. Leave to cool completely.

When you are ready to assemble the dessert, take the custard and cream out of the fridge. Lay the 3 cooled puff pastry sheets on a clean work surface. Pipe half the custard on to one of the pastry sheets in lengthways strips, and place a second sheet of pastry on top. Pipe on the cream in lengthways strips and place the third sheet of pastry on top of the cream. Pipe the rest of the custard on top, and smooth it with a palette knife. Sprinkle with almonds and dust with icing sugar.

PEARS IN RED WINE

We have just spent the weekend helping our father harvest pears at his home in Rutland. This is a perilous task, as the pear tree is high and its branches are infested by hungry wasps and even the occasional hornet. However, a basket of delicious Comice pears was successfully saved from the wasps and a fine pot of pears in red wine was made to celebrate. You can serve the pears with a spoonful of vanilla ice cream if you like.

SERVES 6

6 pears
1 litre red wine
2 sticks of cinnamon, broken in half
2 vanilla pods, cut in half lengthways
2 star anise
2 cloves
100g caster sugar
6 tablespoons crème fraîche

FOR THE CRUMBLE
8 plain digestive biscuits
50g unsalted butter,
cut into small cubes
1 tablespoon icing sugar

To make the crumble, preheat the oven to 180°C/350°F/gas 4 and line a baking tray with baking parchment. Lay the biscuits on top, scatter over the butter and sift over the icing sugar. Bake in the oven for 3 minutes, then remove and allow to cool. Crumble the mixture with your hands and set aside.

Peel the pears, then cut in half lengthways and remove the cores carefully with a small knife. Put the wine, cinnamon, vanilla pods, star anise, cloves and sugar into a large pan and bring to the boil. Add the pears and cook for 15 to 20 minutes, or until tender.

Remove the pears from the pan with a slotted spoon and set aside. Simmer the remaining wine to reduce it by one third – it should lightly coat the back of a spoon – and return the pears to the liquid.

Serve the pears warm or cold, with a dollop of crème fraîche and a sprinkle of the crumble.

RHUBARB SALAD

There is something wonderfully exciting about the arrival of the first of the new season's rhubarb. It must be because it is the first burst of colour to grace the kitchen after the long, drab months of winter. Be careful when cooking the rhubarb that you don't overdo it or the whole lot will turn to mush.

SERVES 4

1 litre orange juice
50ml brandy
1 stick of cinnamon
1 vanilla pod
1 star anise
1kg rhubarb, cut into 5cm lengths
200ml double cream
200g caster sugar
25g softened unsalted butter

Preheat the oven to 140°C/275°F/gas 1. Put the orange juice, brandy, cinnamon, vanilla pod and star anise into a large pan, bring to the boil, then simmer until reduced by half. Add the rhubarb and continue to cook for 2 to 3 minutes, until soft. Remove from the heat and set aside to cool, then remove the rhubarb from the juice with a slotted spoon.

Whisk the cream with 100g of the sugar until it holds soft peaks. Set aside.

Beat the remaining sugar with the butter. Spread on a non-stick baking tray and bake in the oven for 8 minutes.

To serve, divide the rhubarb between 4 glasses, spoon the whipped cream on top and sprinkle the buttery sugar on top of that.

SANTIAGO TART 2010

This is our favourite pudding, both at Barrafina and at Fino. Here's the 2010 version.

SERVES 12

FOR THE PASTRY

115g icing sugar
350g plain flour
215g unsalted butter, cut into small cubes
3 free-range egg yolks
butter, for greasing the tin
plain flour, for dusting

FOR THE FILLING

180g quince paste
250g whole blanched almonds
20ml Amaretto liqueur
zest of 3 oranges
zest of 3 lemons
juice of 1 orange
juice of 1 lemon
115g icing sugar
225g unsalted butter
3 free-range egg yolks
2 free-range eggs

To make the pastry, put the icing sugar and flour into a food processor and start to blend slowly. Add the butter, making sure it is well integrated. Add the egg yolks and pulse until the mixture clumps together. Remove it to a board and bring it together with your hands. Wrap it in clingfilm and refrigerate overnight.

Preheat the oven to 160°C/300°F/gas 4. Grease a 30cm tart tin with butter and dust it with flour. Flour a work surface, then roll out the pastry into a large circle 2mm thick and lay it in the tin, leaving the excess overhanging. Prick the base all over with a fork. Place the tin on a baking tray, then cut out a large disc of baking parchment just a little larger than the tin and place on top of the pastry. Weight down with baking beans.

Bake in the oven for 15 to 20 minutes, or until the edges of the pastry start to turn golden. Remove from the oven, remove the parchment and beans and allow to cool. Carefully trim any excess pastry from the rim of the tart, leaving the tart tin on the baking tray. Turn the oven down to 160°C/300°F/gas 2.

To make the filling, melt the quince paste with 2 tablespoons of water in a bowl over a pan of simmering water. Spread evenly over the tart base.

Put the almonds, Amaretto and orange and lemon zest and juice into a blender or food processor and pulse quickly, keeping the mix quite chunky. Spoon it out, scraping the sides of the bowl with a spatula, and set aside. Add the icing sugar and butter to the blender or processor and whiz to a creamy consistency.

Add the almond mixture to the creamed butter and blend slowly until totally integrated. Add the egg yolks, one at a time, followed by the whole eggs. Spoon the mixture into the pastry case and bake for 40–45 minutes, then dust with icing sugar and serve.

STRAWBERRIES WITH JUANOLA SAUCE

Juanolas are palate-cleansing pastilles made of unsweetened liquorice sold in the pharmacies of Spain. This palate-cleansing effect leads to the intensification of the flavour of the strawberries and makes for a surprisingly pleasant combination. You can use unsweetened liquorice if a Spanish pharmacy is not close at hand. At Barrafina we get our Spanish team to stock up on them when they're in Spain. If you have any juanola sauce left over it will keep for ages in the fridge.

SERVES 4

40g juanolas or soft liquorice
150ml water
30g caster sugar
400g strawberries, hulled and halved
8 fresh mint leaves, finely sliced
sifted icing sugar, for dusting

FOR THE VANILLA CREAM
125ml double cream
25g icing sugar
seeds from ½ a vanilla pod

First make the vanilla cream. Whip the cream in a bowl with the icing sugar and vanilla seeds until it starts to become firm. Refrigerate until needed.

To make the juanola sauce, put the juanolas into a small pan with the water and sugar and bring to the boil. Lower the heat and simmer until the juanolas have dissolved, then continue to simmer until the liquid is reduced by two-thirds and is quite thick. If any undissolved bits remain, pass the liquid through a sieve. Set aside to cool.

Put the strawberries and most of the mint leaves into a bowl with about 80ml of the juanola sauce and stir well.

Place a spoonful of strawberries into a small glass, top with the vanilla cream and serve at once, sprinkled with the rest of the mint.

SUMMER BERRY SALAD WITH MARJORAM VINAIGRETTE

As with all food shopping, choosing the finest ingredients is more important than slavishly sticking to the recipe. For this salad choose the best fruit you can find. Leaving the dressing to stand overnight makes all the difference to this wonderful and exotic dessert.

SERVES 4

250ml double cream
50g icing sugar, sifted
seeds from 1 vanilla pod
150g blueberries
150g raspberries
150g strawberries,
hulled and finely sliced
1 ripe mango, stone removed,
peeled and finely sliced
2 tablespoons caster sugar
8 fresh mint leaves

FOR THE DRESSING
4 tablespoons extra virgin olive oil
1 teaspoon sherry vinegar
juice of 2 limes
1 vanilla pod, split lengthways
a bunch of fresh marjoram

Make the dressing the day before you need it. Put the olive oil, sherry vinegar and lime juice into a bowl and add the vanilla pod and marjoram. Mix well, cover with clingfilm and refrigerate overnight.

Whisk the cream with the icing sugar and vanilla seeds in a large mixing bowl until it starts to become firm. Put into the fridge until you need it.

To serve, divide the fruit between 4 bowls and arrange prettily. Sprinkle with a little caster sugar. Remove the vanilla pod and marjoram from the vinaigrette and drizzle over the fruit. Spoon a little of the cream over the fruit and sprinkle with the fresh mint.

PINEAPPLE SORBET

This is simple, refreshing and easy to make. Try to juice your own pineapple if you can – the fresh juice will taste much better. You will need a juicer for this, but if you don't have one, buy the best pineapple juice you can find.

SERVES 8

300g caster sugar
475ml water
1 large pineapple, juiced, or 400ml good shop-bought pineapple juice
juice of 1 lime

Put the sugar and water into a small pan and heat gently until the sugar has dissolved. Bring to the boil, then turn off the heat. Set aside to cool.

Pour the pineapple juice into a bowl and add the lime juice. Add the syrup, stir well, and churn in an ice cream maker. Once frozen, transfer the sorbet to a plastic container and put into the freezer.

If you don't have an ice cream maker, put the mixture into a plastic container in the freezer and stir every 10 to 15 minutes with a fork to break up the ice crystals, until the sorbet is fully frozen.

Remove the sorbet from the freezer about 15 minutes before you need it, so that it can soften slightly.

SOFT TURRÓN ICE CREAM

Made with almonds, honey and eggs, turrón comes from Alicante and is eaten as a sweet all over Spain, particularly at Christmas time – and very good it is too. It also works very well as an ice cream. If you can't find soft turrón you can substitute another soft nougat.

SERVES 8

500ml full-fat milk
500ml single cream
150g soft turrón, crumbled
6 free-range egg yolks
130g caster sugar

Put the milk, cream and turrón into a large bowl and set aside, covered, for 2 hours or overnight in the fridge.

Put the egg yolks and sugar into a large bowl and whisk together until pale and creamy.

Gently heat the milk mixture in a medium pan until just beginning to steam, then whisk it into the eggs, making sure the milk is not too hot or it will cook the eggs. Leave to cool completely, then churn in an ice cream maker. Once frozen, transfer the ice cream to a plastic container and put into the freezer.

If you don't have an ice cream maker, put the mixture into a plastic container in the freezer and stir every 10 to 15 minutes with a fork to break up the ice crystals, until the ice cream is fully frozen.

Remove the ice cream from the freezer about 15 minutes before you need it, so that it can soften slightly.

WHITE CHOCOLATE AND SAFFRON ICE CREAM

We don't usually go in for much in the way of molecular gastronomy, preferring to leave it to the specialists in the field, but occasionally we dabble our toes in for the fun of it. This unusual combination works very well – just don't be tempted to put in any more saffron.

SERVES 8

50g caster sugar
5 free-range egg yolks
500ml full-fat milk
120ml single cream
8 strands of saffron
250g good-quality white chocolate, broken into small pieces

Whisk the sugar and egg yolks together in a bowl until creamy.

Put the milk, cream and saffron into a small pan and heat gently until just steaming. Whisk the hot milk into the eggs and sugar, making sure the milk is not too hot or it will cook the eggs.

Put the chocolate into a mixing bowl and slowly whisk in the milk mixture, melting it as you go. Leave to cool completely, then churn in an ice cream maker. Once frozen, transfer the ice cream to a plastic container and put into the freezer.

If you don't have an ice cream maker, put the mixture into a plastic container in the freezer and stir every 10 to 15 minutes with a fork to break up the ice crystals, until the ice cream is fully frozen.

Remove the ice cream from the freezer about 15 minutes before you need it, so that it can soften slightly.

LIST OF SUPPLIERS

BRINDISA
The Floral Hall
Stoney Street
Borough Market
London SE1 9AF
tel: 020 7407 1036
website: www.brindisa.com
email: shop@brindisa.com
The best Spanish delicatessen in the UK. You can buy all your cold meats, chorizo, morcilla, oils, vinegars, cheeses, olives, rice, saffron, paprika and much more here. Visit the shop in London or contact their London warehouse (tel: 020 8772 1600, email: sales@brindisa.com) for information about stockists in your area.

L. BOOTH
WILD MUSHROOM COMPANY
Arch 3
Rochester Walk
Borough Market
London SE1 9AF
tel: 020 7378 8666
Can provide you with calçots in season, and wild mushrooms.

CITY MEAT
421 Kings Road
London SW10 0LR
tel: 020 7352 9894
An excellent Spanish butcher supplying milk-fed lamb, suckling pig and special flour for frying.

GARCÍA AND SONS
248–250 Portobello Road
London W11 1LL
tel: 020 7221 6119
website: www.garciacafe.co.uk
A good general Spanish delicatessen.

PUGH'S PIGLETS
Bowgreave House Farm
Garstang Road
Preston
Lancashire PR3 1YE
tel: 01995 601728
website: www.pughspiglets.co.uk
email: pughs@btconnect.com
There are many suppliers of suckling pig in the UK but most tend to have slightly larger piglets (10–12kg) than are used in Spain. Pugh's Piglets has piglets from 5kg.

ONLINE SUPPLIERS

BATH PIG CHORIZO
www.thebathpig.com
Great British-made chorizo.

DON QUIJOTE
www.donquijoteltd.com

FAMILY OPTICA
www.familyoptica.com
Sells Juanola tablets.

HAM LOVERS
www.hamlovers.co.uk
A good range of jamón and cold meats.

HUNTSHAM COURT FARM
www.huntsham.com
Richard Vaughan's outstanding rare breed meat.

QUINTESSENTIALLY GOURMAND
Tel: 020 7498 7089
website:
www.quintessentiallygourmand.co.uk
Fantastic online shop selling Pyrenean milk-fed lamb and suckling pig.

THE TAPAS LUNCH COMPANY
www.thetapaslunchcompany.co.uk

SHERRY

Sherry is good value and widely available. Manzanilla La Gitana – our favourite – is available in most supermarkets. For more serious stuff it is hard to beat Lustau – available at Waitrose and many other good wine merchants. All good wine merchants will stock great sherry and should be able to provide some advice too.

INDEX

Page references for photographs are in **bold**

A

ajillo 206
ajo blanco 153
    lamb cutlets with ajo blanco and black olives 153
    mackerel with grapes, apple
        and ajo blanco 56, **57**
alioli 207, **207**
    crisp fried baby artichokes with alioli 188, **189**
    grilled quail with alioli 116
almonds 18
    delicias 31
    romesco sauce 214
    Santiago tart 2010 **232**, 233
anchovies
    baby gem salad with anchovy
        and pancetta 174, **175**
    crisp fried anchovies 32, **33**
    marinated anchovies with a red onion,
        mint and parsley salad **58**, 59
    skate with black olives, pinenuts
        and anchovies 68, **69**
apples: mackerel with grapes, apple
    and ajo blanco 56, **57**
Arrocina beans with chorizo, morcilla and
    pork belly **128**, 129, **130**
arroz campero **156**, 157
artichokes
    baby artichokes with jamón 187
    confit artichokes **216**, 217
    crisp fried baby artichokes with alioli 188, **189**
    diver-caught scallops with Jerusalem artichoke
        and jamón purée 84, **85**
    Jerusalem artichoke and jamón purée 215
    sea bass with piquillo sauce and
        Jerusalem artichokes **66**, 67
asparagus 18
    asparagus with Payoyo cheese and
        Pedro Ximénez vinegar 185
    white asparagus with romesco sauce 184
aubergines
    grilled aubergines with crisp fried courgettes 197
    pisto and duck egg **200**, 201
avocados: guacamole mousse 72

B

baby artichokes with jamón 187
baby gem salad with anchovy
    and pancetta 174, **175**

baby red mullet with celery salad **46**, 47
Barrafina seafood soup 106–7, **107**, **108**, **109**
basil: langoustines with tomato and basil 102, **103**
beans
    Arrocina beans with chorizo, morcilla
        and pork belly **128**, 129, **130**
    broad beans and goat's cheese on toast **28**, 29
    cuttlefish with runner beans and chickpeas 83
    razor clams with broad beans and jamón 92, **93**
beef
    beef stew **122**, 123
    cecina 43
    fillet of beef with caramelized onions 120
beetroots
    beetroot salad with hazelnut dressing 178
    beetroot salad with Picos cheese **176**, 177
bisque **210**, 211
black pudding see morcilla
blueberries: summer berry salad with
    marjoram vinaigrette **236**, 237
brains: crisp fried milk-fed lamb's brains
    with a spicy tomato sauce 160
braised leg of milk-fed lamb
    with manzanilla 150, **151**
bream: pan-fried whole sea bream 64, **65**
brill
    brill with garlic and lemon 50, **51**
    fritura **76**, 77
broad beans
    broad beans and goat's cheese on toast **28**, 29
    razor clams with broad beans and jamón 92, **93**

C

cabbages
    Hispi cabbage with pancetta 196
    loin of venison with red cabbage,
        pinenuts and sultanas **158**, 159
calçots 18
    calçots with romesco sauce **190**, 191
calves' liver with celeriac purée
    and caramelized onions **162**, 163
capers: octopus with capers **38**, 39
carpaccio: scallop carpaccio 88, **89**
cauliflower: pork cutlets with
    cauliflower purée **136**, 137
cavolo nero: turbot with cavolo nero 75
cecina: hake with fresh peas and cecina **52**, 53

celeriac
    calves' liver with celeriac purée
        and caramelized onions **162**, 163
    celeriac purée 198
    Iberian pig's cheeks with celeriac purée
        and parsnip crisps 132, **133**
celery: baby red mullet with celery salad **46**, 47
ceps: squid stuffed with ceps and prawns **78**, 79
chanterelles: courgette flowers with chanterelles,
    prawns and a spicy tomato sauce 194, **195**
cheese
    asparagus with Payoyo cheese and
        Pedro Ximénez vinegar 185
    beetroot salad with Picos cheese **176**, 177
    broad beans and goat's cheese on toast **28**, 29
cherry catalana 221
chicken
    chicken with romesco sauce **114**, 115
    chicken stock 208, **209**
    chicken wings with garlic and lemon 112, **113**
chickpeas
    chickpeas, spinach and pancetta 192, **193**
    cuttlefish with runner beans and chickpeas 83
chicory
    John Dory with a fennel, chicory
        and radish salad 55
    mojama, chicory and pomegranate salad 182, **183**
chipirones 30
chocolate
    chocolate mousse **222**, 223
    chocolate tart 224
    white chocolate and saffron ice cream 241
choricero peppers 18
    romesco sauce 214
chorizo 43
    Arrocina beans with chorizo, morcilla and
        pork belly **128**, 129, **130**
    chorizo, potato and watercress salad **146**, 147
    txistorra with duck egg and baby potatoes **144**, 145
clams
    clams a la plancha 91
    monkfish tails with seafood rice 63
    razor clams with broad beans and jamón 92, **93**
coca: spinach, pinenut and raisin coca **202**, 203
cochefrito **142**, 143
cod
    cod with a warm salad of lentils
        and mojama **48**, 49

    salt cod fritters with tartare sauce 40, **41**
cold meats 43
confit artichokes **216**, 217
    baby artichokes with jamón 187
    crisp fried baby artichokes with alioli 188, **189**
courgettes
    courgette flowers with chanterelles, prawns
        and a spicy tomato sauce 194, **195**
    grilled aubergines with crisp fried courgettes 197
    pisto and duck egg **200**, 201
crab on toast 101
crema catalana 220
    cherry catalana 221
crisp fried anchovies 32, 33
crisp fried baby artichokes with alioli 188, **189**
crisp fried milk-fed lamb's brains with a
    spicy tomato sauce 160
croquetas
    ham croquetas 34, **37**
    prawn croquetas 35
cuttlefish with runner beans and chickpeas 83

D

dates: delicias 31
deep-frying 14, 17
delicias 31
desserts
    cherry catalana 221
    chocolate mousse **222**, 223
    chocolate tart 224
    crema catalana 220
    macedonia 225
    mil hojas 226, **227**
    pears in red wine **228**, 229
    pineapple sorbet 238, **239**
    rhubarb salad 230, **231**
    Santiago tart 2010 **232**, 233
    soft turrón ice cream 240
    strawberries with juanola sauce 234, **235**
    summer berry salad with
        marjoram vinaigrette **236**, 237
    white chocolate and saffron ice cream 241
diver-caught scallops with Jerusalem artichoke
    and jamón purée 84, **85**
duck eggs
    pisto and duck egg **200**, 201
    txistorra with duck egg and baby potatoes **144**, 145

E

eggs
   alioli 207, **207**
   classic tortilla **164, 166**, 167
   jamón and spinach tortilla 168, **171**
   morcilla, piquillo peppers and quail's eggs 148, **149**
   morcilla tortilla 169, **171**
   pisto and duck egg **200**, 201
   prawn and piquillo tortilla 170, **171**
   txistorra with duck egg and baby potatoes **144**, 145
empanadillas: queen scallop empanadillas with
   red onion and mint salad **86**, 87
escabeche
   quail in escabeche **118**, 119
   tuna in escabeche **70**, 71

F

fennel
   John Dory with a fennel, chicory
     and radish salad 55
   milk-fed lamb's kidneys with onions and fennel 161
fillet of beef with caramelized onions 120
fish
   baby gem salad with anchovy
     and pancetta 174, **175**
   baby red mullet with celery salad **46**, 47
   brill with garlic and lemon 50, **51**
   cod with a warm salad of lentils and mojama **48**, 49
   crisp fried anchovies 32, **33**
   fritura **76**, 77
   hake with fresh peas and cecina **52**, 53
   John Dory with a fennel, chicory
     and radish salad 55
   mackerel with grapes, apple and ajo blanco 56, **57**
   marinated anchovies with a red onion, mint
     and parsley salad **58**, 59
   mojama, chicory and pomegranate salad 182, **183**
   monkfish with new potatoes and spinach 60, **61**
   monkfish tails with seafood rice 63
   pan-fried whole sea bream 64, **65**
   salt cod fritters with tartare sauce 40, **41**
   sea bass with piquillo sauce and
     Jerusalem artichokes **66**, 67
   skate with black olives, pinenuts
     and anchovies 68, **69**
   tuna in escabeche **70**, 71
   tuna tartare 72
   turbot with cavolo nero 75
   see also seafood
fritura **76**, 77

G

garlic
   ajillo 206
   alioli 207, **207**
   brill with garlic and lemon 50, **51**
   chicken wings with garlic and lemon 112, **113**
   romesco sauce 214
goat's cheese: broad beans and goat's
   cheese on toast **28**, 29
grapes: mackerel with grapes, apple
   and ajo blanco 56, **57**
green peppers
   mussels with pepper vinaigrette 94, **95**
   pisto and duck egg **200**, 201
grilled aubergines with crisp fried courgettes 197
grilled lobster 97, **98, 99**
grilled quail with alioli 116
guacamole mousse 72

H

hake with fresh peas and cecina **52**, 53
ham croquetas 34, **37**
hazelnuts: beetroot salad with hazelnut dressing 178
Heritage tomato salad **180**, 181
Hispi cabbage with pancetta 196

I

Iberian pig's cheeks with celeriac purée
     and parsnip crisps 132, **133**
Ibérico meats 18, 43
ice cream
   soft turrón ice cream 240
   white chocolate and saffron ice cream 241

J

jamón 43
   baby artichokes with jamón 187
   diver-caught scallops with Jerusalem artichoke
     and jamón purée 84, **85**
   ham croquetas 34, **37**
   jamón and spinach tortilla 168, **171**
   Jerusalem artichoke and jamón purée 215
   razor clams with broad beans and jamón 92, **93**

fruit
   macedonia 225
   see also individual fruits
fuet de Catalunya 43

Jerusalem artichokes
    diver-caught scallops with Jersualem artichoke
        and jamón purée 84, **85**
    Jerusalem artichoke and jamón purée 215
    sea bass with piquillo sauce and
        Jerusalem artichokes **66**, 67
John Dory with a fennel, chicory
    and radish salad 55
juanolas 17
    strawberries with juanola sauce 234, **235**

K

kidneys: milk-fed lamb's kidneys
    with onions and fennel 161

L

lamb
    braised leg of milk-fed lamb
        with manzanilla 150, **151**
    crisp fried milk-fed lamb's brains
        with a spicy tomato sauce 160
    lamb cutlets with ajo blanco and black olives 153
    milk-fed lamb's kidneys with onions and fennel 161
    rump of lamb with red wine sauce 154
langoustines with tomato and basil 102, **103**
lemons
    brill with garlic and lemon 50, **51**
    chicken wings with garlic and lemon 112, **113**
lentils: cod with a warm salad of lentils
    and mojama **48**, 49
lettuces: baby gem salad with anchovy
    and pancetta 174, **175**
liquorice: strawberries with juanola sauce 234, **235**
liver: calves' liver with celeriac purée
    and caramelized onions **162**, 163
lobsters
    Barrafina seafood soup 106–7, **107**, **108**, **109**
    grilled lobster 97, **98**, **99**
loin of venison with red cabbage, pinenuts
    and sultanas **158**, 159
lomo Ibérico 43

M

macedonia 225
mackerel with grapes, apple and ajo blanco 56, **57**
mangoes: summer berry salad with
    marjoram vinaigrette **236**, 237

manzanilla sherry: braised leg of milk-fed lamb with
    manzanilla 150, **151**
marinated anchovies with a red onion,
    mint and parsley salad **58**, 59
marinated olives 24
marjoram: summer berry salad with
    marjoram vinaigrette **236**, 237
mil hojas 226, **227**
milk-fed lamb's kidneys with onions
    and fennel 161
mint
    marinated anchovies with a red onion,
        mint and parsley salad **58**, 59
    queen scallop empanadillas with red onion
        and mint salad **86**, 87
mojama 18
    cod with a warm salad of lentils and mojama **48**, 49
    mojama, chicory and pomegranate salad 182, **183**
monkfish
    Barrafina seafood soup 106–7, **107**, **108**, **109**
    fritura **76**, 77
    monkfish with new potatoes and spinach 60, **61**
    monkfish tails with seafood rice 63
morcilla 43
    Arrocina beans with chorizo, morcilla
        and pork belly **128**, 129, **130**
    arroz campero **156**, 157
    morcilla, piquillo peppers and quail's eggs 148, **149**
    morcilla tortilla 169, **171**
Moscatel vinegar 17
mousse
    guacamole mousse 72
    chocolate mousse **222**, 223
mullet: baby red mullet with celery salad **46**, 47
mushrooms
    arroz campero **156**, 157
    courgette flowers with chanterelles, prawns
        and a spicy tomato sauce 194, **195**
    squid stuffed with ceps and prawns **78**, 79
mussels
    monkfish tails with seafood rice 63
    mussels with pepper vinaigrette 94, **95**
    mussels in spicy tomato sauce 96

N

nougat: soft turrón ice cream 240

O

octopus with capers **38**, 39
olive oil 17

olives 18
  crisp fried milk-fed lamb's brains with
    a spicy tomato sauce 160
  lamb cutlets with ajo blanco and black olives 153
  marinated olives 24
  skate with black olives, pinenuts
    and anchovies 68, **69**
onions
  calves' liver with celeriac purée and
    caramelized onions **162**, 163
  classic tortilla **164**, **166**, 167
  fillet of beef with caramelized onions 120
  jamón and spinach tortilla 168, **171**
  marinated anchovies with a red onion,
    mint and parsley salad **58**, 59
  milk-fed lamb's kidneys with onions
    and fennel 161
  morcilla tortilla 169, **171**
  prawn and piquillo tortilla 170, **171**
  queen scallop empanadillas with red onion
    and mint salad **86**, 87
  see also calçots
oxtail
  oxtail with scallops 126, **127**
  slow-cooked oxtail **124**, 125

P
paletilla Ibérico 43
pan con tomate 26, **27**
pan-fried whole sea bream 64, **65**
pancetta
  baby gem salad with anchovy
    and pancetta 174, **175**
  chickpeas, spinach and pancetta 192, **193**
  delicias 31
  Hispi cabbage with pancetta 196
  squid wrapped in pancetta with ink sauce 80, **81**
papas a lo pobre 198, **199**
paprika 18
parsley
  ajillo 206
  marinated anchovies with a red onion,
    mint and parsley salad **58**, 59
  parsley oil **70**, 71
parsnips: Iberian pig's cheeks with celeriac purée
  and parsnip crisps 132, **133**
Payoyo cheese: asparagus with Payoyo cheese
  and Pedro Ximénez vinegar 185
pears in red wine **228**, 229
peas: hake with fresh peas and cecina **52**, 53

Pedro Ximénez vinegar 17
  asparagus with Payoyo cheese and
    Pedro Ximénez vinegar 185
  Pedro Ximénez reduction 206
peppers 18
  morcilla, piquillo peppers and quail's eggs 148, **149**
  mussels with pepper vinaigrette 94, **95**
  pisto and duck egg **200**, 201
  prawn and piquillo tortilla 170, **171**
  romesco sauce 214
  sea bass with piquillo sauce and
    Jerusalem artichokes **66**, 67
Picos de Europa cheese: beetroot salad
  with Picos cheese **176**, 177
pig's trotter fritters 134–5, **135**
pimientos de Padrón 24
pineapple sorbet 238, **239**
pinenuts
  loin of venison with red cabbage,
    pinenuts and sultanas **158**, 159
  skate with black olives, pinenuts
    and anchovies 68, **69**
  spinach, pinenut and raisin coca **202**, 203
piquillo peppers 18
  morcilla, piquillo peppers
    and quail's eggs 148, **149**
  prawn and piquillo tortilla 170, **171**
  sea bass with piquillo sauce and
    Jerusalem artichokes **66**, 67
pisto and duck egg **200**, 201
pomegranates: mojama, chicory and
  pomegranate salad 182, **183**
pork
  Arrocina beans with chorizo, morcilla
    and pork belly **128**, 129, **130**
  cochefrito **142**, 143
  cold meats 18, 43
  Iberian pig's cheeks with celeriac purée and
    parsnip crisps 132, **133**
  pig's trotter fritters 134–5, **135**
  pork cutlets with cauliflower purée **136**, 137
  roast leg of Middle White pork **138**, 139
  suckling pig 140, **141**
  see also chorizo; jamón; morcilla; pancetta
potatoes
  chorizo, potato and watercress salad **146**, 147
  classic tortilla **164**, **166**, 167
  jamón and spinach tortilla 168, **171**
  monkfish with new potatoes and spinach 60, **61**
  morcilla tortilla 169, **171**
  papas a lo pobre 198, **199**

prawn and piquillo tortilla 170, **171**
txistorra with duck egg and baby potatoes **144**, 145
prawns
    Barrafina seafood soup 106–7, **107**, **108**, **109**
    bisque **210**, 211
    courgette flowers with chanterelles,
      prawns and a spicy tomato sauce 194, **195**
    fritura **76**, 77
    monkfish tails with seafood rice 63
    prawn croquetas 35
    prawn and piquillo tortilla 170, **171**
    prawns a la sal **104**, 105
    squid stuffed with ceps and prawns **78**, 79

Q
quail
    grilled quail with alioli 116
    quail in escabeche **118**, 119
quail's eggs: morcilla, piquillo peppers
    and quail's eggs 148, **149**
queen scallop empanadillas with red onion
    and mint salad **86**, 87
quinces: Santiago tart 2010 **232**, 233

R
rabbit
    arroz campero **156**, 157
    rabbit stew 155
radishes: John Dory with a fennel,
    chicory and radish salad 55
raisins: spinach, pinenut and raisin coca **202**, 203
raspberries: summer berry salad with
    marjoram vinaigrette **236**, 237
razor clams with broad beans and jamón 92, **93**
red cabbage: loin of venison with red cabbage,
    pinenuts and sultanas **158**, 159
red mullet: baby red mullet with celery salad **46**, 47
red onions
    marinated anchovies with a red onion,
      mint and parsley salad **58**, 59
    queen scallop empanadillas with red onion
      and mint salad **86**, 87
red peppers
    mussels with pepper vinaigrette 94, **95**
    pisto and duck egg **200**, 201
    see also piquillo peppers
rhubarb salad 230, **231**
rice 18
    arroz campero **156**, 157

monkfish tails with seafood rice 63
roast leg of Middle White pork **138**, 139
romesco sauce 214
    calçots with romesco sauce **190**, 191
    chicken with romesco sauce **114**, 115
    white asparagus with romesco sauce 184
rump of lamb with red wine sauce 154
runner beans: cuttlefish with runner beans
    and chickpeas 83

S
saffron 17
    white chocolate and saffron ice cream 241
salads
    baby gem salad with anchovy
      and pancetta 174, **175**
    baby red mullet with celery salad **46**, 47
    baby spinach salad 139
    beetroot salad with hazelnut dressing 178
    beetroot salad with Picos cheese **176**, 177
    chorizo, potato and watercress salad **146**, 147
    cod with a warm salad of lentils and mojama **48**, 49
    Heritage tomato salad **180**, 181
    John Dory with a fennel, chicory
      and radish salad 55
    marinated anchovies with a red onion,
      mint and parsley salad **58**, 59
    mojama, chicory and pomegranate salad 182, **183**
    queen scallop empanadillas with red onion
      and mint salad **86**, 87
salchichón Ibérico 43
salt 17
    prawns a la sal **104**, 105
salt cod fritters with tartare sauce 40, **41**
Santiago tart 2010 **232**, 233
sauces
    ajillo 206
    alioli 207, **207**
    juanola sauce 234, **235**
    romesco sauce 214
    spicy tomato sauce 160, 194, **195**
    squid ink sauce 212
    tartare sauce 40, **41**
    veal sauce 213
scallops
    diver-caught scallops with Jerusalem artichoke
      and jamón purée 84, **85**
    oxtail with scallops 126, **127**
    queen scallop empanadillas with red onion
      and mint salad **86**, 87
    scallop carpaccio 88, **89**

sea bass with piquillo sauce
    and Jerusalem artichokes **66**, 67
sea bream: pan-fried whole sea bream 64, **65**
seafood
    Barrafina seafood soup 106–7, **107**, **108**, **109**
    bisque **210**, 211
    chipirones 30
    clams a la plancha 91
    courgette flowers with chanterelles, prawns
        and a spicy tomato sauce 194, **195**
    cuttlefish with runner beans and chickpeas 83
    diver-caught scallops with Jerusalem artichoke
        and jamón purée 84, **85**
    fritura **76**, 77
    grilled lobster 97, **98**, **99**
    langoustines with tomato and basil 102, **103**
    monkfish tails with seafood rice 63
    mussels with pepper vinaigrette 94, **95**
    mussels in spicy tomato sauce 96
    octopus with capers **38**, 39
    oxtail with scallops 126, **127**
    prawn croquetas 35
    prawn and piquillo tortilla 170, **171**
    prawns a la sal **104**, 105
    queen scallop empanadillas with red onion
        and mint salad **86**, 87
    razor clams with broad beans and jamón 92, **93**
    scallop carpaccio 88, **89**
    squid ink sauce 212
    squid stuffed with ceps and prawns **78**, 79
    squid wrapped in pancetta with ink sauce 80, **81**
sherry 21
    braised leg of milk-fed lamb
        with manzanilla 150, **151**
sherry vinegar 17
skate with black olives, pinenuts
    and anchovies 68, **69**
slow-cooked oxtail **124**, 125
sobresada de Mallorca 43
soft turrón ice cream 240
sorbets: pineapple sorbet 238, **239**
soups: Barrafina seafood soup 106–7, **107**, **108**, **109**
spicy tomato sauce: courgette flowers
        with chanterelles, prawns and a
        spicy tomato sauce 194, **195**
spinach
    baby spinach salad 139
    chickpeas, spinach and pancetta 192, **193**

jamón and spinach tortilla 168, **171**
monkfish with new potatoes and spinach 60, **61**
spinach, pinenut and raisin coca **202**, 203
squid
    Barrafina seafood soup 106–7, **107**, **108**, **109**
    chipirones 30
    fritura **76**, 77
    squid ink sauce 212
    squid stuffed with ceps and prawns **78**, 79
    squid wrapped in pancetta with ink sauce 80, **81**
stocks
    bisque **210**, 211
    chicken stock 208, **209**
    veal stock 213
strawberries
    strawberries with juanola sauce 234, **235**
    summer berry salad with
        marjoram vinaigrette **236**, 237
suckling pig 140, **141**
    cochefrito **142**, 143
sultanas: loin of venison with red cabbage,
    pinenuts and sultanas **158**, 159
summer berry salad with
    marjoram vinaigrette **236**, 237

T

tartare sauce 40, **41**
tarts
    chocolate tart 224
    Santiago tart 2010 **232**, 233
tempura 194, **195**
tomate frito 18
tomatoes
    courgette flowers with chanterelles, prawns
        and a spicy tomato sauce 194, **195**
    crisp fried milk-fed lamb's brains
        with a spicy tomato sauce 160
    Heritage tomato salad **180**, 181
    langoustines with tomato and basil 102, **103**
    mussels in spicy tomato sauce 96
    pan con tomate 26, **27**
    romesco sauce 214
tortillas 165
    classic tortilla **164**, **166**, 167
    jamón and spinach tortilla 168, **171**
    morcilla tortilla 169, **171**
    prawn and piquillo tortilla 170, **171**

tuna
   cod with a warm salad of lentils and mojama **48**, 49
   mojama 18
   mojama, chicory and pomegranate salad 182, **183**
   tuna in escabeche **70**, 71
   tuna tartare 72
turbot
   fritura **76**, 77
   turbot with cavolo nero 75
turrón: soft turrón ice cream 240
txistorra with duck egg and baby potatoes **144**, 145

V

vanilla cream 234, **235**
veal
   calves' liver with celeriac purée and
      caramelized onions **162**, 163
   rump of lamb with red wine sauce 154
   veal sauce 213
venison: loin of venison with red cabbage,
   pinenuts and sultanas **158**, 159
vinaigrette
   mussels with pepper vinaigrette 94, **95**
   summer berry salad with
      marjoram vinaigrette **236**, 237
vinegar 17
   asparagus with Payoyo cheese and
      Pedro Ximénez vinegar 185
   Pedro Ximénez reduction 206

W

watercress: chorizo, potato and
   watercress salad **146**, 147
white asparagus 18
   white asparagus with romesco sauce 184
white chocolate and saffron ice cream 241
wine
   pears in red wine **228**, 229
   rump of lamb with red wine sauce 154

ACKNOWLEDGEMENTS

We would all like to thank Emma Lee for the fabulous photos and constant good humour. Thanks also to all at Fig Tree, especially our editors, Juliet Annan and Jenny Lord, for their sage advice and tireless product research. Many thanks also to John Hamilton, Penguin's art director, and to Nathan Burton for his excellent design. And a big thank you to our agent, Simon Benham, for bringing welcome rock and roll to the book industry.

SAM: as ever all love and thanks to my brilliant wife Robin and our three amazing children, Freddie, Thomas and Sophie. To all the team at Barrafina, Fino and Quo Vadis – your perpetual efforts are much appreciated. And finally to Nieves – you brighten our day with your fabulous cooking!

EDDIE: to Nieves, without whose creativity, passion, drive and dedication this book would have never come to fruition. To Nieves's friendship and loyalty. To my brother Sam, who makes every work-day together a joy and inspiration.

NIEVES: thanks to Sam and Eddie for trusting in me to open Barrafina and for my involvement in this book. A big thank you to all the team at Barrafina both past and present, especially Alicia Maria Hernández, Tomasz Baranski, Darío, Jon, David, García, José, John, Toni, Aga, Gossia and Carlos. Also many thanks to the team at Fino for all their support, especially Samuel, Saber, Maden, Kaska, Martin, Seb and Anna. To my parents, Maria Nieves Mohacho and Pedro Barragán, many thanks for all their wonderful support over the years. It gives me great pleasure to make them proud. And finally to all the Barrafina customers – your continued support is much appreciated.